Kevin Belton's
BIG FLAVORS
OF NEW ORLEANS

Kevin Belton's BIG FLAVORS of New Orleans

KEVIN BELTON with RHONDA K. FINDLEY

PHOTOGRAPHS BY DENNY CULBERT

GIBBS SMITH
TO ENRICH AND INSPIRE HUMANKIND

First Edition
20 19 18 17   11 10 9 8 7

Text © 2016 Kevin Belton with Rhonda K. Findley
Photographs © 2016 Denny Culbert

Published by
Gibbs Smith
P.O. Box 667
Layton, Utah 84041

1.800.835.4993 orders
www.gibbs-smith.com

Designed by Katie Jennings Design
Printed and bound in Hong Kong
Gibbs Smith books are printed on paper produced from sustainable PEFC-
certified forest/controlled wood source. Learn more at www.pefc.org.

Library of Congress Cataloging-in-Publication Data

Belton, Kevin, author.
  Kevin Belton's big flavors of New Orleans / Kevin Belton with Rhonda
K. Findley ; Photographs by Denny Culbert. — First Edition.
     pages cm
  Includes index.
  ISBN 978-1-4236-4157-5
1. Cooking, American—Louisiana style. 2. Comfort food—Louisiana—
New Orleans. I. Title.
  TX715.2.L68B445 2016
  641.59763—dc23
                    2015028095

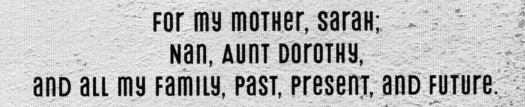

For my mother, sarah;
nan, aunt dorothy,
and all my family, past, present, and future.

CONTENTS

8 · Acknowledgments

11 · The Flavors of New Orleans:
    A Neighborhood Experience

14 · Roux

16 · The Trinity

18 · Classic New Orleans

24 · Jazz Brunch

30 · Rice Favorites

35 · Traditional Mexican

41 · Soul Food

47 · Mom's Saturday Staple

53 · New Year's Inspiration

58 · German Heritage

63 · Shrimp Specialties

69 · Egg Dishes

76 · Classic Creole

82 · Italian Influences

87 · Gettin' Crabby

93 · Trio of Soups

100 · Down-Home

107 · Carnival

114 · Fresh Catch

120 · French Beginnings

126 · Oysters

132 · Thanksgiving

138 · Wash Day

144 · Garden Harvest

149 · Potatoes

154 · Poultry

159 · Irish New Orleans

164 · Reveillon Dinner

170 · Resources

171 · Index

ACKNOWLEDGMENTS

IT WAS A COMPLETE JOY WORKING ON this book with my friend Rhonda. Getting the voices in my head all together, I am sure, was like herding cats for her. We spent many hours eating and laughing at ourselves.

Thanks to Monica. She was able to keep us in line and on schedule so she could edit all our screw ups.

My cousin Lorna enabled me to recall memories and thoughts accurately. Many thanks to Austin, Cabral, and Packy for the work they put in prepping and organizing so all I had to do was walk in and not mess it up. With Denny's amazing eye, he was able to bring our creations alive on the plate. So not only did they taste wonderful, they looked wonderful as well.

It was a pleasure working with Terri, Dawn, and Jim and the entire staff at WYES (PBS New Orleans) in being able to share New Orleans' food and culture with others.

The New Orleans School of Cooking was founded in 1980 by Joe Cahn because there was nowhere people could go to learn about New Orleans' cuisine. Thanks to the efforts of Greg and Suzanne, the school is still a family-run business. We get to introduce New Orleans' food and culture to people around the world. Bruce Trascher was not only a fellow chef and business partner, but most of all, he was my friend and I miss him very much.

—Kevin

Thank you Kevin, for believing in our partnership and trusting me with your family memories and food secrets. Because of you and your family, this book is filled with love. Monica, you make us all look good. Carlos Leon, your support means the sky is the limit. Thank you Fatma for letting us sit for hours on end in Fatoush while we wrote and ate your amazing food.

—Rhonda

THE FLAVORS OF NEW ORLEANS: A NEIGHBORHOOD EXPERIENCE

I GREW UP AT 2719 VALENCE STREET in Uptown New Orleans. That makes me an Uptown New Orleans boy. My parents, Sarah and Oscar Belton, along with my Grandmother Nan, created a true, comfortable home where family, food, and love were the main ingredients. That's actually a New Orleans home to me. Looking back now, I've come to realize that our household truly reflected the values and the personality of what it means to be from New Orleans.

Our house was in the New Orleans style called a double shotgun, with a few minor architectural changes à la Miss Magnolia Battle's discretion. That's my Grandmother Nan for ya.

Shotgun style means the rooms in a house line up one after another with no hallway and are pretty open for everyone to know everybody's secrets. So you get pretty close. And, we liked it like that. Up until I was six or seven years old, Nan and I were roommates. She was my best friend, mentor, teacher, and overall life coach. It was by her suggestion that my parents added on the upstairs addition called a camelback that became my childhood oasis.

The kitchen was the heart and soul of our house. The rich yellow walls were offset with white trim. The shiny, white porcelain sink was perfection, not a scratch on it. The appliances sparkled. You could eat off my mom's kitchen floor. We gathered together around the kitchen table everyday for almost every meal.

I was ringside for all family discussions that took place at that table. Whether we were talking about current events or work issues or the needs of family and friends, those issues were taken up usually over shelling pecans, stirring the gumbo pot, cooking rice, or peeling shrimp.

I suppose that's why I feel most comfortable in the kitchen. Any kitchen. Your kitchen. My kitchen. That's what comfort is to me. Laughter. Tears. The smell of gumbo cooking. And, love. Lot's of love. And lots of food.

My parents were adventurous and weren't shy about getting out in the city. Intrinsically, New Orleanians are very neighborhood-centric. That's still true to this day. Not the Belton clan. We were out and about all over town in search of great food and, of course, family visits. We had family and friends all over the city—the 7th Ward, New Orleans East, Westbank, the French Quarter, where my dad lived until about age 10. I mean all over. So I like to say that I experienced New Orleans from the backseat of a blue 1960 Dodge Dart. And, those experiences with my family made me the person and the chef I am today.

As an only child, I shared the backseat of the Dart, driven by my mother, with the bounty of fresh ingredients from markets, grocers, and butchers from across the city. My mom knew the very best spots to shop for the freshest ingredients city-wide.

We would get fresh shrimp from the seafood lot over in Westwego. Mom would drive across the Mississippi River Bridge back in those days when there was only one bridge downtown. Often times, I hit the open lot market with her. And, other times, she would drop me off at Sid Goodreaux's house to socialize while she ran to the market. Mom was not afraid to power over to the Westbank if that meant getting fresh-caught seafood. I shared the backseat with shrimp that was still wiggling fresh from the water or blue crabs packed in ice. On the way back, she would stop at Don's Seafood on Broad Street for fresh oysters. They'd come along for the ride in the backseat, too.

Mom was committed to fresh food. I realize this now because of how she managed the kitchen and me and Dad as well. It wasn't unusual for Mom to be cooking dinner and turning on her heels and saying, "Can you run over and get some French bread?" She only had to ask once. Dad and I were up and out the door for a quick run up Freret Street and over to Simon Bolivar to the front door of Leidenheimer's bakery for fresh French bread. It seemed like they never turned off the ovens there. I remember the little retail store. And, the flashing red light indicating that a new, fresh batch of bread was just out of the oven.

Getting fresh bread was that quick in New Orleans. That easy. And, I just always thought that's what everybody else did. We never went for just one loaf, it was always two. The Belton men would snack on one on the way home.

Trips to see my Grandma Emily and Grandpa Oscar along with Uncle Norman and Aunt Marion in the 7th Ward usually were intertwined with a visit to the butcher for the best Creole sausage in New Orleans. For me, the 7th Ward was all about butchered meats and handmade sausages as well as the best fried-oyster po'boy in the city. Again, Mom had figured out who did the best and I'm grateful that she always took me along to experience these places first hand.

Not 10 minutes from the house, in front of the seminary on Carrollton Avenue, the produce man parked on the side of the street advertising his fresh produce. Mom and I were regulars. Over the years, I learned about Louisiana seasonal produce and how to choose ripe fruits and vegetables. Snapping. Thumping. Smelling. Inspecting. All skills my mother possessed and passed along to me in subtle ways right there in the middle of the bustling traffic. I can still see her face as she took great joy visiting and shopping.

Around the corner from the house on Freret Street was our local bakery, Long's. I loved their donuts. The glazed and jelly were my two favorites. When Mom was running her errands and we were close to Toledano around Washington in Central City, a stop at Gambino's for Doberge and rum cake was always on her list.

It was rare that we ate out in restaurants. Mom had mastered most of the dishes that make New Orleans cuisine remarkable. I guess she, Dad, and Nan figured why go out and be disappointed when Mom was the master of all the New Orleans foods we loved.

With that being said, there were a few spots that got my mother's attention. Dooky Chase, ground zero for Creole cuisine, created by Chef Leah Chase, being one of those spots. I remember going to Dooky Chase with Mom, Dad, Aunt Dorothy, Lorna, and Chet. Things that stood out to me as a kid were Chef Leah's stuffed shrimp and gumbo. Eddie's on Law Street also made the list of restaurants my Mom enjoyed with us. We ordered their seafood dishes. And, of course, Chez Helene, off St. Bernard Avenue around North Robertson and Laharpe, for the fried chicken and stuffed bell peppers by Chef Austin Leslie. Eating Chef Austin's food is one of my favorite food memories of all time.

Today, my mantra about New Orleans is the one my parents and grandparents taught me as a child. When you live in a city, use the whole city. The Beltons were not afraid to venture out for the best food and the best ingredients. The butchers. The oyster shuckers. The seafood vendors. The department managers at Schwegmanns. These were important people in our lives.

I raised my two sons, Kevin and Jonathan, the same way my parents and grandparents raised me, around the table. I wanted them to understand how special New Orleans is and show them the places where we shopped and the neighborhoods where our families lived. And, that meant going all over and eating everything in sight. We went across the lake on big food adventures. A lot of times they would ask me, "Why are we going to the grocery store across the river?" I'd say, "Well, its part of our city, too."

I think Kevin channels my Uncle Chet for sure. My Uncle Chet was Mom's fresh fish provider. Today, Kevin is known for dropping a line every chance he gets, just like Uncle Chet did. And, Kevin often cooks at home with his wife, Christina. It is such a joy for me to visit with them and my grandson Carter in Lafayette, Louisiana, and watch them in the kitchen. I feel so proud. It takes me back to the kitchen on Valence Street.

Jonathan is my roommate these days. And, I feel so lucky for that. He brings groceries home and the bags seem to always be from different stores, just like my mother shopped. So all the influences I conveyed seemed to rub off on them. These little actions keep our family culinary traditions alive, and at the same time, New Orleans culinary traditions alive and well, too.

Kevin's favorite dish of mine is gumbo and that means with potato salad. Jonathan is a fan of my alligator sauce piquante. He actually asked me to cook a huge batch of it for his friends as a high school graduation present. That pretty much sums up how we Beltons feel about food. I'm proud of the fact that they both are pretty good cooks, too.

I shop from the Westbank to Metairie. I eat Uptown, Downtown, and everywhere in between. I shop in New Orleans East at the Vietnamese Market and the Holly Grove Farmers Market. I'm not shy about pulling over on Claiborne Avenue to buy a fresh melon off the back of a truck. I will drive thirty minutes to try a new restaurant. I'm thrilled when a new chef arrives in New Orleans and receives national acclaim for using New Orleans ingredients in a different way. And, I continue to thrive on teaching daily classes on gumbo, jambalaya, and roux techniques to the thousands of students who attend The New Orleans School of Cooking classes in the heart of the French Quarter. We did the math the other day and figured I have taught over 500,000 students to this day and counting. That's a lot of people getting the good word on the hallmark dishes of New Orleans. Every time I think about it, I'm just so proud.

I've come to realize New Orleans is just one big neighborhood. Lots of cities in the United States have history. Here in New Orleans,

we've kept our history alive. Our food and recipes stayed the same over time. There aren't many places that have embraced and kept their history alive in the same way we have here. I'm proud to be a Creole New Orleanian. I'm certainly proud of my culinary heritage. Life here truly revolves around the table.

Little did I know that all of the food adventures and the neighborhood adventures my family took me on were preparing me for life as a chef and an educator. Those same ingredients I shared the backseat with as a child have become the key ingredients in my life and my career.

ROUX

It's R-O-U-X, not rue as in a New Orleans street name. A roux is one of the fundamental cooking elements of New Orleans cuisine.

The French roux was butter and flour cooked for about five minutes or so just to get rid of the flour taste. That's called a blonde roux. This blonde roux is the base for many of the French sauces like a Béchamel, the mother of all classic sauces.

Here in New Orleans, someone made a decision in a Creole kitchen to go past the five minutes to see what happened to the roux. And, the result was one of the distinctive flavor elements for our cooking techniques in the Crescent City.

How do you make a roux? Well, that's both an easy and complicated question. A roux can be what you want it to be or even what you simply need it to be to reach your flavor expectation.

For instance, think about a piece of bread toasting in the same way as cooking a roux. As bread toasts it gets to different stages of flavor. Cooks realized the longer the roux was stirred over the heat it took on different stages of flavor as well.

The most important thing about cooking a roux is that it is tended constantly. By tending constantly, I mean you stir the entire pan, not particularly fast, just consistently, and you incorporate the entire contents of the pan from the bottom up.

Simply put, the roux has to be stirred. And every nook and cranny in the pan needs to be stirred. Oh, and you cannot walk away. Trust me. I know. Which leads me to a funny story.

As a child growing up in New Orleans, you had time to get away with whatever you wanted to do when Mom was making a roux. She couldn't walk away from the roux for at least 10 minutes. Not having anyone to chase or run from, as an only child, my choice of shenanigans while Mom was stirring the roux was bed jumping. A past time, by the way, I gave up when I started breaking the slats at about eight years old. True story—I knew how much I could get away with by smelling the roux cooking. As soon as I knew Mom started the roux, off I'd run to my makeshift trampoline. I would smell the roux cooking and could tell when she was almost finished by the nutty aroma. The smell was my cue. I learned to smell when a roux was done, well before I learned the visual cue of a finished roux.

So you ask what does a perfect roux look like? Well, I'm going to tell you that it depends. Pretty crazy, huh? Because, that is one of the beautiful things about a roux. It's truly personal. Think of gravy. Your grandma makes a light gravy for mashed potatoes. But your mom makes a brown gravy for her mashed potatoes. They both taste amazing. But they looked completely different. So apply that same perspective to gumbo. I make dark, chocolate-colored roux for gumbo. It doesn't matter if it's delicate seafood or duck with andouille sausage. My gumbo is dark because my flour and oil combination is cooked completely toasted, if you will. The color change comes from the flour actually cooking. Flour only cooks in a fat. So butter or oil is the fat you need to make a roux. If you like a very dark roux then you have to use a high heat oil that can withstand the cooking time. If you are going for a lighter roux then butter is what you use.

Yes. New Orleans flavors come from fat. Accept it. Embrace it. And, enjoy the flavor. The color changes the longer you cook the roux over the heat. Of course, the darker the roux, the more intense and complex the flavor and the longer you have to stir. From a light blonde-colored roux or a peanut butter colored-roux to a dark, chocolate-colored roux, these are the color ranges you pass through during the process. Remove your roux from the heat, and it basically stops cooking. You decide.

Also, the pan you cook the roux in matters, too. No Teflon coated pans. You can't tell if the roux scorches. It's better to toss a burnt roux and start over than toss out a pot of gumbo.

So my advice is to practice. Experiment. Enjoy. And, turn off your phone. Put the dog out. Give your kids something to do and make your roux.

——— THE TRINITY ———

When you are looking for the main flavor in New Orleans cooking, you won't find it in a shaker, a container, a bottle, or a box. The flavor is actually from the moisture that comes from cooking with onions, celery, and green bell pepper.

Classical French cooking relies on the use of a *mire poix* which is two parts onion, one part celery, and one part carrot. The problem was there were no carrots in south Louisiana 300 years ago. What we had here in New Orleans were plenty of bell peppers.

So the onions, celery, and bell peppers became the New World mire poix ingredient combination that is the foundation of most of New Orleans signature dishes—soups, sauces, stocks, and main dishes. All of them rely on the Creole mire poix to build the flavor. A general mire poix can be different depending on the culture. And, as one can surmise, here in New Orleans, our cuisine referred to French techniques because that's who settled here first. The industrious settlers and cooks in Louisiana incorporated the bell pepper out of necessity and created a unique flavor profile that is recognized as the only non-Native American indigenous cuisine in the United States—Creole cooking.

The addition of the bell pepper adds a third vegetable that sweats just like the onion and celery and adds even more moisture when cooked in the oil. Carrots are a dryer ingredient and more subtle in complexity. The bell pepper is so in your face. And, more moisture, in this case, with the ingredient tweak means more flavor. That flavor is completely different and extraordinarily unique from classic French cooking. The new combination was created out of necessity, but is now integral to the flavor profile of New Orleans cuisine.

Being a predominately Catholic settlement, whether under French rule or Spanish, it is interesting to note that the same religion, Catholicism, guided the city for so many years under the concept of the Holy Trinity, the big three of the Catholics. The name stuck for the big three of New Orleans cuisine. It would be sacrilege not to cook with the traditional three: onions, celery, and bell pepper.

Because the trinity is such a foundation of New Orleans cooking, Mom often would start sautéing onions, celery, and bell pepper before she decided what she was actually cooking for dinner.

When you are going for true Creole flavor, be sure to invite the trinity into the pot. Onions, celery, and bell pepper, because you can't cook New Orleans food without them.

Classic New Orleans

When I talk about classic New Orleans recipes, what comes immediately to my mind are not only the expected dishes like red beans and rice, jambalaya, gumbos, and the like, I'm also thinking about the neighborhoods and families and what you find in the culturally diverse kitchens throughout the City. I can write a whole book on this subject. When I started to think about the main dishes and the soups and the side dishes of New Orleans, the list literally became miles long. So I just wanted to pick out a few things that I felt embodied the food expectation that people have whether they are a neighbor or a friend or a visitor to New Orleans. These are the dishes that people are intrigued by. A dish they've heard of and expect to have a certain flavor or look. And, they expect to eat and experience while in the city.

The *maque choux* for example. Do you learn how to pronounce it first? Or do you just eat it and worry about pronouncing it later? But, seriously, this dish is a perfect classic New Orleans food. The name seems French or Creole and the components are from a dish made by the local Native American Indians who grew the corn. You find it served with fish and fried chicken. And, it's classic and ancient in the way that it represents an example of a recipe that has survived over the years and hasn't really changed much from the original interpretation.

When you go out to eat in different parts of New Orleans, in different restaurants, you will find the same certain dishes on the menu. These dishes have possibly been around as long as this city has been around. It could be a side like Corn Maque Choux. Or, it could be a restaurant's version of gumbo, which there are more versions of than street names here. And, of course, you really shouldn't leave New Orleans without having a beignet.

French Quarter Beignets

The iconic fried donut à la New Orleans. It was wonderful as a child being handed the powdered sugar and given the go-ahead to sprinkle the sugar without any limits. Oh man, heaven.

Serves 4 to 6

---

1 cup warm water

¾ cup sugar, divided

¼ ounce (1 package) active dry yeast

2 large eggs, beaten slightly

1¼ teaspoons salt

1 cup evaporated milk

6½ cups all-purpose flour, divided

¼ cup shortening

2 cups powdered sugar

Combine water, ¼ cup sugar, and yeast in a large bowl and let set for 10 minutes. You can start this in your stand mixer, if you have one, or use a large bowl.

In a separate bowl, whisk the eggs. Add salt, milk, and remaining sugar. Add the egg mixture to the yeast starter. Add 3 cups flour and combine thoroughly. Cut in the shortening and continue to mix. Add remaining flour and mix to form a large dough ball.

Flour your work surface and knead the dough until smooth, about 10 minutes. Place dough into a large bowl, cover, and place in a warm place to rise, about 2 hours.

When ready to fry, heat oil in deep fryer to 350 degrees.

Roll out the dough ¼ inch thick and cut 2-inch squares. Fry to a golden brown, turning continuously. Remove and drain on paper towels. Sprinkle with powdered sugar and serve hot with extra powdered sugar, of course!

TIPS & SUGGESTIONS

You can make this dough ahead of time, let it rise, and then refrigerate. It holds great for two or three days wrapped in plastic wrap. You can freeze it, too. Quarter the dough and wrap each section. Just remove, thaw, and fry.

seafood gumbo

One might think seafood, with its delicate, unique flavors, would be overpowered adding it into a heavy, rich, and dark roux. It isn't. The crabs, shrimp, and oysters love to flutter around in that dark pool of goodness. I use okra to thicken and stay with a dark roux to ensure the all-around rich expectation of this dish. **Serves 8 to 10**

---

1 pound fresh okra, cut into quarters

2 1/2 quarts fresh seafood stock

2 bay leaves

1 cup vegetable oil

1 1/4 cups all-purpose flour

1 1/2 cups chopped onion

3/4 cup chopped green bell pepper

3/4 cup chopped celery

3 tablespoons Creole seasoning

1/2 teaspoon cayenne pepper

3 pounds (16/20 shrimp), peeled and deveined with tails on

1 pound fresh crab claws

1/2 pound fresh crabmeat

1 pound smoked sausage, cut in rounds about 1/4-inch thick, optional

Kosher salt and pepper, to taste

4 cups cooked white rice

1/2 cup chopped green onions

Preheat oven to 375 degrees. Place okra in a Dutch oven and roast, uncovered. Okra will begin to weep and become thick and stringy. Continue to bake until the stringy texture cooks away, about 30 minutes. Remove from oven and set aside.

In a large stockpot, bring the seafood stock to a boil over medium-high heat. Add bay leaves.

In a large skillet, start your roux by heating vegetable oil on medium heat. Stirring continuously, sprinkle in flour until your mix is the consistency of wet sand. Continue to cook and stir until the roux is a dark peanut butter color.

Add the onions and cook for 5 minutes. Add bell pepper and celery and continue to cook until vegetables soften, another 4 minutes. Sprinkle in Creole seasoning and cayenne pepper and stir to fully incorporate. Cook for 1 minute.

Add roux and vegetables to stock and mix thoroughly. Bring to a boil and simmer for about 30 minutes.

Add shrimp, crab claws, crabmeat, and sausage, if using. Cook for an additional 5 minutes. Serve over rice and garnish with green onions.

TIPS & SUGGESTIONS

If you have trouble finding fresh shrimp for this recipe, you can use the precooked frozen. We won't tell. Just add them at the end of the recipe. They just need to be in the gumbo long enough to heat through. If you cook them too long, they can become rubbery. Just keep your eye on them.

CORN MAQUE CHOUX

I remember my first taste of corn cut fresh from the cob. I can clearly see my mom going to the trouble of shucking and trimming. I wondered why she didn't just open a can or a freezer bag. Well, let me tell you why. There is nothing better than fresh corn off the cob. Nothing whatsoever. **Serves 4 to 6**

---

3 ears corn, husks and silks removed

2 tablespoons butter

$\frac{1}{2}$ cup chopped yellow onion

$\frac{1}{4}$ cup chopped green bell pepper

1 teaspoon Creole seasoning

1 teaspoon fresh thyme

1 tablespoon minced garlic

$\frac{1}{2}$ teaspoon hot sauce

3 stalks green onion, chopped

$\frac{1}{4}$ cup chopped fresh tomato

Italian parsley, to taste

$\frac{1}{4}$ cup heavy cream

$\frac{1}{2}$ teaspoon kosher salt

$\frac{1}{2}$ teaspoon white pepper

Roast corn until heated through, about 10 minutes on a roaster, or in a 400 degree oven for 10 minutes on a roasting rack. Remove from oven, cool, and remove corn from the cob. Set aside.

In a large skillet, heat butter and sauté the corn, onion, bell pepper, Creole seasoning, thyme, garlic, hot sauce, green onion, tomato, and parsley. Cook until soft, about 10 minutes.

Add cream and continue to cook for 2 minutes. Remove from heat and add salt and pepper. Adjust seasoning and serve warm.

TIPS & SUGGESTIONS

If you can't get fresh corn then use frozen. If you have to resort to a canned corn, I'd just say don't make it.

Jazz Brunch

The brunch culture that began in the French Quarter was started by an industrious culinarian by the name of Madam Begue. She had a place right across from the French Market where Tujaques is today on Decatur Street. She would do these huge spreads where the French Market workers gathered around noon to have their huge meal after working the Market and docks in the early morning hours. At the end of their day, which was late morning, the workers were ready for a hearty meal that paralleled with breakfast. Being a practical woman, I guess she figured she would do both, breakfast and lunch. And, viola she invented the brunch.

I can remember Mom using the term brunch one day. I asked her, "What's the deal with the brunch thing?" She explained to my young mind that when you ate a little later you could have breakfast and lunch at the same time. That sounded pretty good to me, of course.

I remember my cousin Lorna talking about meeting up with her friends and going to jazz brunch. Food and music together just makes sense in New Orleans, right? I fondly remember my first jazz brunch at Commander's Palace, and sitting out on the patio room with the glass roof. I was probably still in high school. Lorna was working in New York and Chet was in school at Harvard and back for a visit . . . so off to jazz brunch to celebrate. My mother's idea of jazz brunch was eating a late breakfast at home. So I learned to do both.

When I partnered with Wayne Baquet at Li'l Dizzy's Café on Poydras Street, the second location, we did a huge Sunday jazz brunch. It lasted a good part of the day. Most of the time people would be coming in after mass—those were the early folks. Other churches would get out later, about noon or so. We stayed busy all day and every Sunday.

I consider the jazz brunch in New Orleans a ritual of sorts. It brings the three great things about our city together—food, people, and music. From the classic jazz brunch born at Brennan's on Royal Street to the gospel brunches, it's one of New Orleans' expected culinary events. I always tell people when they come to New Orleans for the weekend, make sure to fly out Sunday night. Otherwise, you'll miss brunch!

new Orleans Bananas Foster

I love this dessert because it's almost like a breakfast dessert. The warm sauce and ice cream are a perfect finish to a long brunch with family. At jazz brunch, in particular, it's not uncommon for the musicians to stroll around. Equally as common is Bananas Foster made tableside. The whole dish, including the tableside preparation, is a culinary flourish à la New Orleans. And, we have Ms. Ella Brennan and the Brennan family to thank for creating this landmark New Orleans dish. **Serves 6**

½ cup butter

½ cup brown sugar

2 teaspoons vanilla

1 teaspoon cinnamon

4 ripe bananas, peeled and sliced on the bias

1 cup dark rum

3 ounces banana liqueur

Vanilla ice cream

In a large skillet over medium heat, melt butter and add brown sugar, vanilla, and cinnamon. Stir with a wooden spoon. Add bananas and cook until caramelized over medium-high heat, about 3 minutes.

Remove pan from heat and add rum and liqueur. With a long lighter, ignite and let flame cook out the alcohol. Flame will die out when alcohol has evaporated.

Spoon hot banana mixture over individual servings of vanilla ice cream and serve immediately.

TIPS & suggestions

Add chopped pecans, about ½ cup, to the butter and brown sugar sauté to add a bit of a nutty flavor. Leftover sauce is great over pancakes the next day.

GRILLADES AND GRITS

This is simply a classic Creole dish. My mother made it. My grandmothers made it. It was a clever way to use scraps of meats or even turn an ordinary cut of meat into something special. Using the Creole trinity to make a hearty gravy and pairing with grits is not an uncommon combination for us Creoles. It's a great hearty dish for brunch. ***Serves 4***

MEAT

8 (4-ounce) pieces of pork or beef cutlets, sliced to $\frac{1}{4}$ inch-thickness

1 cup all-purpose flour

4 tablespoons Creole seasoning

2 tablespoons vegetable oil

GRAVY

$\frac{1}{4}$ cup chopped onion

$\frac{1}{4}$ cup chopped celery

$\frac{1}{4}$ cup chopped green bell pepper

$\frac{1}{2}$ cup diced tomato

4 cloves garlic, peeled and minced

$\frac{1}{4}$ cup vegetable oil

$\frac{1}{4}$ cup all-purpose flour

2 tablespoons red wine

2 teaspoons Worcestershire sauce

$\frac{1}{4}$ teaspoon cayenne pepper

2 bay leaves

$2\frac{1}{2}$ cups beef broth

Kosher salt and freshly ground pepper, to taste

1 cup stone-ground grits, cooked according to package directions

Italian parsley

MEAT

Rinse cutlets, pat dry, and chill in the refrigerator for about 20 minutes. Chilled cutlets fry better.

In a separate bowl, combine flour and seasoning. Dredge cutlets on both sides with the flour. Season all cutlets thoroughly. Set aside.

In a large skillet over medium-high heat, bring oil to temperature. Evenly space cutlets in the pan and cook until thoroughly browned, about 4 minutes on each side. Remove and set aside.

GRAVY

Add onion to the skillet and sauté until translucent, about 5 minutes. Add celery and bell pepper and continue to cook until tender, about 5 minutes. Add tomato and cook for 1 minute. Add garlic and cook until you smell the aroma, about 1 minute. Transfer vegetables from pan and set aside.

Using the same pan, make a roux gravy using the oil and flour. Heat oil and slowly add flour until the consistency is that of wet sand. Continue to stir and cook until roux is a dark brown.

Add wine, Worcestershire, cayenne, bay leaves, and broth. Stir. Add vegetables and stir again. Add cutlets, cover, and reduce heat to a simmer.

Continue to simmer for about 30 minutes or until the grillades are fork tender. Season with salt and pepper.

Serve over grits and sprinkle with parsley.

TIPS & SUGGESTIONS

Polenta works well in place of the grits. Or, serve grillades over mashed potatoes for a great dinner.

PAIN PERDU

In French, pain perdu literally translates to "lost bread." It is called lost bread because the bread has lost its freshness. It was a great morning when all the French bread wasn't eaten the night before. Mom almost always was making traditional lost bread for breakfast. **Serves 4**

---

2 tablespoons butter

5 eggs, whisked

$1/2$ cup whole milk

2 tablespoons sugar

1 teaspoon cinnamon

1 teaspoon nutmeg

$1/2$ teaspoon vanilla

$1/4$ teaspoon kosher salt

8 slices stale French bread, cut on the bias about $3/4$ inch thick

Fresh fruit of choice

Powdered sugar

Honey, maple syrup, or Steen's Pure Cane Syrup

Preheat oven to 200 degrees. Heat butter in a large skillet on medium-high heat.

In a medium bowl, whisk eggs, milk, sugar, cinnamon, nutmeg, vanilla, and salt to form the egg-wash mixture.

Dredge each slice of bread in the egg wash on both sides. Immediately place in skillet and cook on each side until crispy brown, about 2 minutes on each side, turning once. Remove and hold in warm oven on a heatproof plate while cooking the remaining pieces of bread.

Garnish with fresh fruit and powdered sugar. Serve with honey or syrup.

TIPS & SUGGESTIONS

Whatever bread you choose to use in this recipe must be more on the dry side. Drying out the bread allows it to absorb more liquid from the egg wash. Leave bread out overnight and it should be perfect.

Rice Favorites

As a kid, I didn't know why we had rice at every meal. I just knew that we had rice. It wasn't until I got older that I found out Louisiana is ground zero for rice in the United States.

I loved it when Mom would start sautéing onion, celery, and green bell pepper. It just smelled like love. You'd ask what she was making and she'd say, "I don't know yet." And, I believe that to be true. She knew that flavor was important to start with. She was so intuitive with her cooking that getting started meant just that. The beginning of something great from the kitchen was when Mom started to sauté.

There was this certain big pot that lived in our kitchen. That was the designated rice cooking pot. Mom had her own way of cooking rice. She didn't do the traditional two-to-one ratios. She'd just let that rice simmer until she decided it was done. At that point, she would drain off the excess water. Then, she would rinse the rice in cold water to stop it from cooking. The rice would go back into the colander and on hold. When it was time, Mom would put the colander back into the big pot and wait to steam the rice back to temperature for mealtime. Pretty unconventional as rice cooking goes. She truly made the best rice in the world.

Leftover rice was just as valued at our house. Leftover rice would reappear as rice pudding among other things. Both Mom and Grandma Emily made terrific rice pudding. Grandma put cinnamon and raisins in her creation as did Mom. I can't pick a favorite out of the two.

And, I do remember Grandma Emily made calas too, which I think is very cool. In Creole culture, calas are essentially the original street food of New Orleans. African descendents as well as Creole women sold the calas on the streets of the French Quarter. History places these industrious female entrepreneurs outside of the churches on Sunday selling to the Catholics that fasted during the morning before receiving communion. It is noted that many Creole and African women financed their freedom and the freedom of family members through the sale of calas. Powerful.

A cala is a fried-rice fritter or rice cake made with egg, flour, butter, and so on. And, it isn't unusual to find it dusted with powdered sugar. Some say calas were created by Africans who came from rice-producing regions. But the name has a French derivation as well. And, you find a version of it in some Hispanic regions.

I'm so happy that my Creole grandmother was the one who introduced me to calas. They are part of my heritage. The first chef here to reintroduce calas to New Orleans after it all but disappeared from the culinary landscape was Heidi Trull, the founder of the iconic Elizabeth's in the Bywater.

As far as rice goes here in New Orleans, if there is not a pot of rice cooking, someone is going to ask you what's wrong with you. You just better have it.

Traditional New Orleans Calas

The image of Creole women sitting outside the many Catholic churches in the French Quarter with baskets of warm balls of calas made parishioners very happy. There was a time that the rules of the church in this predominantly Catholic city were such that you couldn't eat anything before mass so you were ready to receive communion. Coming out of church and feeling so hungry, the Creole calas were certainly hard to resist. And, these steadfast entrepreneurs used their earning to create a path to freedom. **Makes about 12**

Oil, either peanut or vegetable, for frying

1 cup all-purpose flour

1¼ teaspoons baking powder

½ teaspoon ground cinnamon

½ teaspoon ground nutmeg

½ teaspoon allspice

3 large eggs

¼ cup sugar

2 teaspoons vanilla

½ teaspoon kosher salt

2 tablespoons Steen's Pure Cane Syrup

1½ cups cooked organic long-grain rice, chilled

½ cup powdered sugar

Heat oil for frying to 350 degrees.

Combine flour, baking powder, cinnamon, nutmeg, and allspice; sift thoroughly and set aside.

In a medium bowl, beat the eggs, sugar, vanilla, and salt until foamy and about double in volume, around 2 minutes. Add in ½ of the dry ingredients and continue to mix. Add syrup. Once thoroughly incorporated, add remaining dry ingredients.

Add rice to the wet batter and combine until the mixture just comes together. It should be a loose, rough rice ball.

Scoop out balls of rice batter the size of a golf ball and gently drop into fryer. Continue to add the rice balls, being careful not to overcrowd the fryer. Use a slotted spoon to move the calas around to make sure they cook evenly and turn a golden brown.

Remove from oil and allow to drain on a paper towel. Dust with powdered sugar and serve warm.

TIPS & SUGGESTIONS

Peanut oil is perfect for high-heat frying. If peanut oil is not an option, vegetable oil will give similar results. This recipe easily doubles.

CHEF KEVIN'S JAMBALAYA À LA BIG EASY

The trinity—onions, celery, and bell pepper—make the classic base of this Creole rice dish. Jambon is the French word for ham. Laya is the African word for rice. It loosely translates as "gift of rice" as the dish has evolved with other ingredients and substitutions. At The New Orleans School of Cooking, I believe I've demonstrated how to make jambalaya a million and one times. I'm not kidding. It is the number one requested dish by the visitors to the city. It's interesting from the point of view of a culinarian that this is the only Louisiana dish where the rice cooks with the ingredients. Most Louisiana dishes are created and served over rice. Here rice is the heart. **Serves 4 to 6**

---

1 cup chopped onion

1 cup chopped celery

1 cup chopped green bell pepper

4 tablespoons butter

4 cloves garlic, finely chopped

4 cups chopped chicken, dark meat preferred

1 1/2 pounds smoked beef sausage, cut in 1/2-inch rounds

2 1/2 cups diced fresh tomatoes

2 tablespoons Creole seasoning

2 cups beef broth

1 1/2 cups uncooked long-grain white rice

Kosher salt and pepper, to taste

1/4 cup chopped Italian parsley

1/4 cup chopped scallions

In a large heavy-bottom pot, sauté the onions, celery, and bell pepper in butter over medium heat until the onions are translucent, about 8 minutes. Add garlic and continue to cook for 1 minute or until you can smell the garlic cooking.

Add the chicken and sausage and sauté for 2 minutes. Add the tomatoes and Creole seasoning and sauté for 2 more minutes. Add broth and rice. Stir and bring to a boil. Reduce heat, cover tightly, and simmer until rice is cooked, about 20-25 minutes.

Adjust seasoning with salt and pepper. Stir in parsley and scallions and serve immediately.

TIPS & SUGGESTIONS

It is best to use unflavored long-grain rice.

Kevin's Creole Rice Custard Pudding

My mother didn't make this dish very often since we didn't have a lot of rice leftover. I always had a gut feeling when there seemed to be lots of leftover rice that Mom was craving her own amazing rice pudding. If she didn't have any leftovers, she would cook a pot of rice for her rice pudding. **Serves 4 to 6**

---

2 cups water	2 eggs	1 teaspoon cinnamon
1 teaspoon kosher salt	1 cup sugar	1/2 teaspoon ground cloves
1 tablespoon butter	1 teaspoon vanilla	1 cup dark raisins
1 cup uncooked white rice	1 teaspoon allspice	
1 quart whole milk	1/2 teaspoon nutmeg	

In a large saucepan, bring water to a boil and add salt, butter, and rice. Stir and cover tightly with lid. Reduce heat to a simmer and cook for 15 minutes. Remove from heat, uncover, and fluff rice.

Return the rice to the stovetop over low heat and slowly begin to add the milk, stirring constantly. Bring to a slow simmer. Stir frequently to avoid scorching the milk and allow the rice to slowly absorb the liquid.

In a small bowl, whisk the eggs and sugar lightly until it develops a light-yellow sheen. Add to the simmering rice. Continue to cook until mixture begins to thicken, about 5 minutes. Add vanilla and spices. Stir to blend thoroughly. Add raisins and stir. Remove from heat.

Pour into a shallow 9 x 9-inch glass baking dish and cool to room temperature. Cover tightly and refrigerate until set, about 3 hours. Dust generously with cinnamon and serve chilled.

Tips & Suggestions

This is a terrific way to enjoy leftover rice. You can skip the first step when using 2 cups of leftover rice.

Traditional Mexican

As a kid, the closest thing we had to Mexican food was thanks to Dad. Dad really liked Manuel's Hot Tamales in Mid-City. He would bring tamales home as a treat. And, Mom usually worked them in as a dinner appetizer.

When I was at Brother Martin High School, I was a member of the chorus. We had the opportunity to travel to Mexico for a music festival and we stayed in the Olympic Village just outside of Mexico City. On our way back, we were so lucky to stay a couple of days in Mexico City. That was my first introduction to authentic Mexican cuisine. I can remember the soups, the beans, and traditional rice dishes. Sounds a little like home, huh?

Returning to New Orleans, I realized that Mexican food was an enigma and what I experienced in Mexico was definitely more complex than what I was exposed to. But I didn't give it much thought until . . . Hurricane Katrina.

After Hurricane Katrina, with the influx of so many Latinos and within that influx so many Mexican nationals, New Orleanians could enjoy authentic Mexican cuisine with more accessibility. Food trucks and tiny bodega-style restaurants began to pop up to satisfy a new wave of immigrants. So the renaissance, although wasn't really intended to permeate the food culture, did, and made a significant modern impact. Right around the corner from The New Orleans School of Cooking is one such Mexican restaurant, Felipe's Taqueria. I find myself often just pulling right up to the front door and parking in a loading zone spot on Decatur Street to run in a grab one of the steamed burritos made to order. It's not fancy. It's just really good. And I discovered, by the way, I'm an "Al Pastor" man.

FISH TACOS WITH COASTAL TACO-LADE SAUCE

I am a fan of fish. Growing up eating fresh fish every week, thanks to my Uncle Chet, I appreciated the fresh flavors and the different preparations my mother and grandmother created. The Latino flavors infused in the creation of fish tacos is such a delightful new way to experience fish. **Makes about 12 soft tacos**

---

2 pounds redfish or red snapper filets

3 tablespoons melted butter

6 tablespoons Creole seasoning

12 (6-inch) corn tortillas

Freshly chopped cilantro

Shredded lettuce

Diced avocado

Chopped red onion

Brush filets in butter and coat fish with a thick layer of Creole seasoning. On an extremely hot grill or in a cast iron skillet heated to smoking temperature, cook coated fish until blackened on all sides, about 2 minutes on each side. This can be extremely smoky, so it's great to do this on your outdoor grill.

Remove from grill and set fish aside, covered. Lightly butter corn tortillas and heat on a griddle until warmed, about 1 minute for each tortilla. Turn once after 30 seconds, careful not to burn them.

Cut fish into 1-inch strips and place in tortillas. Add cilantro, lettuce, avocado, and red onion and top with Coastal Taco-lade Sauce.

TIPS & SUGGESTIONS

Any mild, flaky fish works great. Use your favorite. Shrimp is a super substitute or addition to this recipe. Expand the garnishes to include your favorites.

COASTAL TACO-LADE SAUCE

This is just a milder version of the traditional rémoulade. It allows the flavors of the fish and toppings to come through in a New Orleans flavor way. **Makes about 1¼ cups sauce**

2 tablespoons white vinegar or red wine vinegar

1 teaspoon lemon juice

2 tablespoons Creole seasoning

1 tablespoon paprika

1 tablespoon Creole mustard

¼ cup chopped green onions

¼ cup olive oil

Kosher salt, to taste

1 cup mayonnaise

Mix vinegar, lemon juice, Creole seasoning, paprika, mustard, and green onion with olive oil. Add salt. Fold in mayonnaise to desired consistency.

TIPS & SUGGESTIONS

You can use a traditional white or red rémoulade if you prefer a stronger taste. This recipe doesn't require using the entire cup of mayonnaise. Just fold in until you reach your desired consistency. Feel free to make a fresh salsa as well. The salsa and the "taco-lade" actually work rather well together.

CHEF KEVIN'S SUNDAY MORNING CURE (PAZOLE)

As a real New Orleanian, I have never had a hangover. But, I hear from friends that the best thing to eat after a night out listening to live music and indulging in libations is something hearty, warm, and spicy. This pork- and corn-based Latino traditional soup has just enough of a kick to get you back right. **Serves 8**

CHILE SAUCE

1 cup dried chiles de árbol, seeded and stems removed

5 dried ancho chiles, stems removed

4 cloves garlic, smashed

1 teaspoon kosher salt

PAZOLE PORK

1 teaspoon kosher salt

3 teaspoons cumin powder

1 (3-pound) pork roast, trimmed and halved

1 onion, finely chopped

3 tablespoons vegetable oil

4 cloves garlic

10 cups chicken broth

1½ tablespoons dried oregano

2 bay leaves

32 ounces hominy, soaked and cooked

CHILE SAUCE

Layer the chiles in a large, deep pan. Place a heat-proof plate on the chiles to weigh them down and cover with boiling water for about 30 minutes or until fully hydrated. Remove from water. Reserve 1 cup of soaking liquid.

Using a blender, blend the chiles with the soaking liquid until smooth. Add garlic and salt and continue to blend until mixture is smooth.

Strain through a fine sieve into a large bowl. Set aside.

PAZOLE PORK

Combine the salt and cumin and rub generously on the pork roast. In a large soup pot, sauté the onion in the oil until cooked, about 7 minutes. Add the garlic and continue to sauté for 1 minute. Push garlic and onion to one side. Add pork and brown thoroughly.

Add broth, oregano, and bay leaves. Turn up heat to high. Add 1 cup of chile sauce. Bring to a boil then reduce heat to a simmer. Cover loosely and reduce heat to low. Cook for about 2½-3 hours. Turn pork several times. It will be fork tender and easily shred.

Add hominy, and simmer uncovered for about 45 minutes.

TIPS & SUGGESTIONS

This can be made two days ahead of when you want to serve it. A beef roast is a great substitution, if you prefer. It is tasty served with sliced avocado, sour cream, grated cheddar cheese, fresh peppers, red onion, and/or sliced bread.

Traditionally Classic Guacamole

Make it truly Creole by using authentic Creole tomatoes. The spice from this recipe comes from a Louisiana-made hot sauce instead of cayenne. **Serves 4 to 6**

3 avocados, peeled and seeded

½ cup finely chopped red onion

2 tablespoons chopped cilantro

2 fresh whole tomatoes, chopped

2 cloves garlic, minced

1 teaspoon cumin powder

1 teaspoon hot sauce

1 lime, juiced

Kosher salt, to taste

In a medium bowl, mash the avocados, onion, and cilantro to form a paste. Add tomatoes, garlic, cumin, hot sauce, and lime juice. Continue to mash thoroughly. Finish with a sprinkle of kosher salt.

TIPS & SUGGESTIONS

There is never enough. Make extra.

Homemade Tortilla Crisps

It's just a whole, different flavor when you make these fresh at home. It really does not take as much effort as you think. You might never buy a bag of these chips again after tasting the results. **Makes about 48 crisps**

Vegetable oil

12 (6-inch) flour tortillas, each cut into 4 wedges

4 tablespoons butter

1 tablespoon cumin

1 teaspoon kosher salt

Heat oil to 350 degrees in deep fryer.

Gently dip tortilla wedges into hot oil and cook until crispy and golden, about 1 minute. Remove and drain on paper towels.

In a small saucepan, melt butter. Add cumin and salt. Stir to fully incorporate and remove from heat. Brush cooked tortillas with melted butter mixture. Serve hot.

TIPS & SUGGESTIONS

You can make crisps without the oil in a 350 degree oven. Bake tortilla wedges on a cookie sheet until crispy, about 10 minutes. Remove and brush with butter mixture. Serve immediately. With either preparation, if you prefer concentrated flavor, sprinkle additional seasonings on after brushing with butter.

SOUL FOOD

I learned to cook with soul from my mother and my grandmothers.

I didn't exactly know what that meant. I know Mom enjoyed cooking. My grandmother enjoyed that time together in the kitchen. It didn't become clear until I worked with Chef Austin Leslie what soul food actually is. One day he mentioned, "Soul food . . . you gotta put a little of yourself in each dish." At that time it dawned on me, that's what the ladies in my life, and for that fact, most of my relatives did, too.

Chef Austin appeared on a show called *Cooking with Soul* that, at the time, was hosted by Chuck Lampkin. They filmed at The New Orleans School of Cooking's facility at Jax Brewery. I had a front row seat at that table. It was in the mid-90s and I was quick to put myself as close to Chef Austin as I could. I believe he was one of the greatest pure, real chefs to come out of New Orleans, ever.

I also hosted a show for WYES back in 2003 that focused on soul food in New Orleans. When the soul food topic came about, I invited those people whom I considered the soul-food greats of New Orleans to come on the show. Of course, I invited Chef Leah Chase, Wayne Baquet, and Chef Austin. These are the leaders and torchbearers of New Orleans' soul food, real and authentic.

Still to this day, I believe these chefs embody the epitome of New Orleans soul food. Also, I learned that soul food for me isn't a particular type of cuisine. Soul food spans cultures and can be recognized globally. Simply put, soul food is food made with love. It is true comfort food.

Teaching at The New Orleans School of Cooking puts me in direct contact with folks who just love the New Orleans style of cooking. Visitors come up to me all the time and say, "You make it look so easy." Cooking is easy for me. It comes naturally, and most importantly, I enjoy it. And, I get immense pleasure through cooking. The kitchen is where I am most comfortable. But to add to that, showing people how we make New Orleans food is a great joy in my life. I really feel lucky that I'm able to do what I truly love to do. And, I really enjoy sharing the New Orleans food culture.

In New Orleans, the soul in cooking does mean that you are truly putting a little bit of yourself in each dish and sharing that with whomever will enjoy that food with you. The women in my family all did this and I believe that it has made me the person I am today. Soul food is just another term for comfort food plus a dash of yourself.

new orleans-STYLe Fried CHICKen

Crunchy. Moist. Flavor. Done right . . . is New Orleans fried chicken. All this wonderful flavor is simple and good. **Serves 4**

---

1 (3½-pound) fryer chicken

Salt and pepper, to taste

1 egg, lightly beaten

1 cup half-and-half

1 cup water

½ cup all-purpose flour

3 tablespoons Creole seasoning

Vegetable oil

½ cup chopped parsley

Dill pickles

Cut up your fryer, rinse, pat dry, and season with salt and pepper. Chill in refrigerator for an hour.

Whisk egg in a bowl large enough to dip chicken pieces. Add half-and-half, water and season with salt and pepper. Set aside. Combine flour with Creole seasoning in a separate bowl and set aside.

Dip chicken pieces in seasoned flour. Dip in egg mixture. Coat thoroughly. Set all pieces aside. (Just before placing chicken in skillet, dip again in dry seasoning and immediately place in the pan. This keeps the coating from sliding off. If that happens, the crunchy outer layer will not form as gloriously!)

Heat oil in a large skillet, place chicken in hot oil, and brown on all sides. If oil is popping too much outside of the pan, reduce heat a bit. Cook thoroughly, about 10–12 minutes until outer layer is crisp. Garnish with parsley and serve with pickles.

TIPS & SUGGeSTIONS

It's very important to coat the chicken dry, wet, and then dry. You get the very best results. You can also season the chicken the night before and refrigerate as cold as possible. The chicken will fry better cold. If you have a deep fryer, it is a great way to get solid results. If you are using a skillet, you want to start with about an inch of oil and place the big pieces, breast and thighs, in the skillet first, careful not to overcrowd the skillet. If you need to add more oil during the cooking process, that is fine. Just make sure you allow the oil to heat up before adding the next batch of chicken. Also, turn the pieces every couple of minutes as it just helps the cooking process and keeps the chicken from overcooking.

STUFFED GREEN BELL PEPPERS

*This was the trick my mother used to get me to eat vegetables. For me, this dish takes me way back to my mother's kitchen. When she sautéed the meat to brown it off, she would add some shrimp and turn the fire off. The house would smell like her amazing stuffed peppers. She'd add the seasoning and rice and then turn the fire off. I'd always hope she would make more of the stuffing, so I could eat what wouldn't fit in the peppers. The onion, celery, and bell pepper combination is the base for all Creole dishes. This is a great way to showcase the bell pepper on its own. **Serves 4 to 6***

---

8 green bell peppers, tops removed, seeded, and cleaned (chop and reserve tops)

1 tablespoon butter

1 tablespoon olive oil

2 pounds very lean ground beef, cooked

1/2 cup chopped onion

1/2 cup chopped celery

1 1/2 cups diced fresh tomatoes

8 ounces tomato sauce

2 cloves garlic, crushed

2 teaspoons Creole seasoning

1/2 cup chopped fresh basil

2 teaspoons salt, divided

1 egg, whisked

1 teaspoon pepper

2 teaspoons Worcestershire sauce

2 cups cooked long-grain, organic rice

1 cup grated mild cheddar or mozzarella cheese

1/2 cup chopped Italian parsley

Preheat oven to 350 degrees.

Place bell peppers into a large soup pot and cover with salted water; bring to a boil. Boil for 1 minute, reduce heat, and simmer for 7 minutes. Remove from heat, drain, rinse with cold water, and arrange in a shallow baking dish; set aside.

While peppers are cooking, melt butter and olive oil in a large skillet over medium heat, sauté ground beef until cooked, about 5 minutes. Add reserved chopped bell pepper tops, onion, and celery and continue to sauté until the onion is translucent, about 5 minutes. Add tomatoes, tomato sauce, and garlic. Sauté for 2 minutes until you smell garlic cooking. Add Creole seasoning, basil, and 1 teaspoon salt, stir, reduce heat, and simmer for 10 minutes.

In a large bowl, combine egg, remaining salt, pepper, and Worcestershire sauce. Add rice and beef mixture from the skillet. Mix thoroughly and divide equally among the bell peppers.

Pour remaining tomato sauce over peppers. Bake for 1 hour. Top with cheese, place under broiler for 3 minutes or until cheese begins to brown. Garnish with parsley and serve.

TIPS & SUGGESTIONS

You can use other colors of bell peppers, red, yellow, or orange, if available. Also, adding Gulf shrimp after you brown the meat is just an added bonus that really works great and continues the theme of New Orleans ingredients.

sweet potato pie

This is my momma's recipe. It's simple. It's basic. It's straightforward. And, it's what we eat in New Orleans. **Serves 6**

---

1 (9-inch) deep-dish pie crust

6 tablespoons butter, softened

$\frac{1}{2}$ cup sugar

2 eggs

2 large sweet potatoes, boiled, peeled, and mashed.

$\frac{1}{2}$ cup evaporated milk

1 teaspoon vanilla

$\frac{1}{2}$ teaspoon cinnamon

$\frac{1}{2}$ teaspoon allspice

$\frac{1}{2}$ teaspoon nutmeg

$\frac{1}{4}$ teaspoon salt

Whipped cream

Candied pecans

Preheat oven to 425 degrees. Score bottom of pie crust with a fork and set aside.

Cream butter and sugar in a large bowl. Whisk eggs, add to butter mixture, and thoroughly combine. Add sweet potatoes and milk and continue to combine. Add vanilla and spices and mix thoroughly until smooth.

Pour mixture into pie crust (there will be extra filling) and bake for 12 minutes. Reduce heat to 350 degrees and bake 40 minutes more or until knife inserted in center comes out clean.

Serve with whipped cream and a candied pecan garnish.

TIPS & SUGGESTIONS

There will be more filling than what will fit into the pie but not enough for the second pie. That's because Mom always made extra in small Pyrex glass ramekins and put them in a water bath at the same time she made the pie. That way she had organized extras for the next night.

mom's saturday staple

Saturday was an off day from school but a workday around the house. Mom and I made groceries every Saturday. Makin' groceries is a New Orleans phrase for a trip to the grocery store. That phrase was used in an advertising campaign created by the Schwegmann family of grocers. Leave it to New Orleans to make a little distinction for the most mundane like a trip to the grocery store. However in New Orleans, makin' groceries can be an art and even a hobby.

Every Saturday, I knew shopping was on Mom's agenda. Groceries. Sundries. The meat market. Mom also was known to throw in a few surprises. Haircuts sometimes made the list. Back home, I usually had my own list: clean your room, do laundry, cut the grass. And then, pass out!

Mom's favorite Saturday haunts were either Schwegmann's on Broad or their Airline Highway store. After getting what was on the list, we'd go back home and put those away. Then it was off to the meat market.

Mule's was usually number one on her list for meat. Mule's is now known as Bachemin's Meat Market as ownership changed in the late 60s. It sat on St. Bernard Avenue right next to the Circle Food Store. Big green building. Hard to miss.

Mom got all our meats there, veal for the paneed meat, pork chops, steaks. All the meats were hand cut to order. You know, the real deal. Bachemin's Creole hot sausage is the best in the world.

There was always a wait at Bachemin's. So either my mom would bring me across the street to Mr. Royal to get a haircut, or, I got to go into the back and watch them make the hot sausage. Mr. Walter, Bachemin's proprietor, would put me on a stool with a front row seat to the magic. Afterward, we'd run back to the house to put away the meat.

Time to start cleaning. My mom would suggest I go make something to eat. Beans were usually on the stove, but wouldn't be ready until dinner. So left to my own devices, I dispatched a sugar sandwich. Two slices of bread, a thin spread of butter, and a sprinkle of sugar from the container that always set out on the kitchen table. You slap those slices together. Comfort food for a kid. I'm sure many of you remember a sugar sandwich.

I'd come out and my mother would say, "Did you get you something?" I'd smile and say, "Of course." Thank God it's Saturday.

Nan's Saturday Buttermilk Pancakes with Praline Bacon Sprinkles

What kid doesn't want to wake up on Saturday morning to pancakes and cartoons? Of course, chores were on the menu, too. But Nan's pancakes made going to school all week worth it and even the chores, too. The praline bacon is wonderful and adds that certain Louisiana flavor. **Makes about 10 (4-ounce) pancakes**

---

3 cups all-purpose flour

2 teaspoons baking powder

1 teaspoon baking soda

$^1/_2$ teaspoon kosher salt

3 tablespoons sugar

2 large eggs, beaten

4 cups buttermilk

4 tablespoons unsalted butter, melted and cooled, plus 1 teaspoon to coat griddle

1 teaspoon vanilla

1 cup fresh fruit, blueberries, strawberries, or choice

$^1/_2$ cup maple syrup or Steen's Pure Cane Syrup

Preheat griddle to 375 degrees. Preheat oven to 200 degrees.

In a large bowl, thoroughly mix the dry ingredients together. In a separate bowl, combine, eggs, buttermilk, melted butter, and vanilla.

Add egg mixture to dry ingredients and mix through until the flour mixture is completely moistened. Batter should have some lumps. Be careful not to over mix the pancakes or they will not be fluffy. You can use an electric mixer or mix by hand. Either works just as well.

Test griddle by sprinkling a few drops of water to make sure it is at cooking temperature. Brush on butter to prime the griddle top. Wipe off any excess.

Using a 4-ounce ladle, make batter puddles about 4 inches apart on the griddle top. When pancakes begin to bubble in the center and are forming brown, crisp edges, about 2–2 $^1/_2$ minutes, turn and continue to cook for 1 minute. If you are adding the fruit into the pancakes, sprinkle thoroughly with the fruit prior to turning and just before the edges are showing crispiness.

Hold pancakes in the oven on a heatproof plate while continuing to cook the remaining batter.

Serve with more fresh fruit, syrup, and Praline Bacon sprinkles.

Tips & Suggestions

You can use regular milk if you don't have buttermilk. And, add whatever fruit or nuts to the batter you think sounds good. Or, even save your add-ons for a simple topping. Recipe easily doubles.

PRALINE BACON SPRINKLES

Heidi Trull, who created the Bywater restaurant, Elizabeth's, is my hero when it comes to bacon. Her praline bacon is the best I've ever had. I'd never heard of it before her rendition. And, I give great kudos to her for taking the simplicity of bacon and launching it to a new level with the idea of keeping it New Orleans. **Serves 4**

1 pound thick-cut bacon

1 cup brown sugar

$^1/_2$ cup Louisiana pecan pieces

Preheat oven to 350 degrees.

Place bacon strips on baking sheet lined with parchment. Bake for about 10-12 minutes until bacon fat is rendering. Remove from oven, drain fat, and reserve for later use.

Combine the brown sugar and pecans.

Coat the bacon slices generously with the pecan topping. Return to oven and continue to bake until bacon is crispy, about 5-8 minutes. Remove and cool. Serve in strips or as a crumbled topping for your pancakes or even grits.

CHEF KEVIN'S NEW ORLEANS-GLAZED HAM PO'BOYS

Words my mother said to me at the Canal Villerie, another one of our local grocers . . . "Son, grab a half pound of Chisesi, please." "Kevin, we need a whole Chisesi." Or even, "Get a pound of Chisesi, sliced thin." My mother never said, "Get some ham." As far as I knew, Chisesi was ham, the only ham. That's how we are in New Orleans—loyal to our local food traditions.

It wasn't until I was an adult that I figured out that there's ham and then there's Chisesi. For me, it's the pinnacle of ham in New Orleans created by a local company, Chisesi Brothers Meat Packing Company. They've made meats, and in particular, ham for more than 100 years. Yes, ham is ham. But Chisesi is New Orleans' ham. It's comfort food for sure. This recipe starts with a good ham and this glaze and cooking technique creates a delicious baked ham perfect for po'boys. **Makes 4 large or 8 small po'boys**

Ham Glaze

24 ounces quality root beer

2 tablespoons hot-pepper jelly

1 bay leaf

2 tablespoons Caribbean steak sauce, such as Pickapeppa

8 whole cloves

½ stick cinnamon

4 ounces (about 2 tablespoons) freshly squeezed orange juice and zest

½ lemon, zested

Ham Coating

½ cup brown sugar

4 tablespoons Creole mustard

6 ounces quality root beer

¼ cup Steen's Pure Cane Syrup

1 teaspoon allspice

1 (4 to 5-pound) ham, fresh or smoked

Ham Glaze

In a large saucepan, thoroughly combine glaze ingredients, bring to a boil over high heat, and cook for 1 minute. Reduce the heat to a simmer and cook for approximately 25 minutes. You can begin preparations on the ham.

Remove from heat and strain. Return to pan and continue to cook over medium heat until the mixture is reduced by half. It should be the consistency of a thick syrup. Remove from heat and set aside.

Ham Coating

In a large bowl, combine brown sugar, mustard, root beer, syrup, and allspice. Mix well and set aside.

Ham Preparation

Preheat oven to 350 degrees. Line a medium Dutch oven with aluminum foil.

Prepare the ham by scoring a crisscross pattern across the top of the ham. Place in Dutch oven and brush with glaze. By hand, pat on a thick crust of the coating.

Place in the oven, uncovered, and cook for an hour or until the internal temperature of the ham reaches 160 degrees. Every 15 minutes baste the ham with the glaze until mixture is used up, about the 45 minute cooking mark.

Remove from oven and allow the ham to rest for 30 minutes before slicing.

Tips & Suggestions

So the Chisesi brand is totally ingrained in my DNA. But, as a chef, I know there are many other great local ham brands throughout the world. Use your local ham and I'll bet it will be equally as good.

How to Dress a New Orleans Po'Boy

When you come to New Orleans and order a po'boy, you will be asked if you want it dressed. Now you know what it means when someone asks you if you want your po'boy "dressed."

1 loaf French bread

1 cup mayonnaise

24 ounces sliced ham

8 (3-ounce) slices cheese, cheddar is preferred but any cheese is fine

8 tomato slices

2 cups shredded iceberg lettuce

Cut the bread loaf in half and smother with the mayonnaise. Layer on the remaining ingredients. Cut into 4 large or 8 small po'boy sandwiches. Enjoy with a cold root beer.

MISS Magnolia BaTTLe's SOUTHern-STYLe BUTTer Beans

My Grandmother Nan's given name is Magnolia Battle. Doesn't that just ooze character and charm? Believe me; she lived up to her name. There was just something about the creaminess of the butter bean after Nan cooked it. The smell and the flavors just take me way back to our kitchen on Valance Street. **Serves 6 to 8**

---

1 (16-ounce) package dried butter beans

1 cup chopped onion

4 tablespoons butter

8 ounces pickled meat, cut into chunks

4 cups vegetable stock

4 cups chicken stock

1 bay leaf

1 teaspoon kosher salt

1 teaspoon freshly ground pepper

Rinse and soak beans, covered, for about 4 hours in the refrigerator. Or overnight, if possible.

In a large heavy-bottom saucepan, sauté onion in butter until translucent, about 5 minutes. Drain beans. Add pickled meat and beans. Combine vegetable and chicken stocks in a pitcher. Add enough combined stock to cover the beans and add bay leaf.

Bring the beans to a slow boil, reduce heat, and simmer. Cover pot loosely. Check every 15 minutes to add stock to just cover the beans. Resist the urge to stir the beans as it will cause the tender beans to split apart. Continue to check the liquid level and cook for about $1\frac{1}{2}$ hours. Season with salt and continue to simmer until beans are tender, about an additional 30 minutes.

Gently remove beans to a serving dish and discard meat. Season with salt and pepper, gently stirring, and serve.

TIPS & SUGGeSTIONS

Find that fine line of stirring to keep the beans from sticking but not over-stirring to the point where the tender bean falls apart. I really don't mind if the butter beans split apart a little bit. That just adds to the creaminess. Find the balance that works for you.

New Year's Inspiration

Mom cooked the classics to ring in the New Year. Cabbage and black-eyed peas. I have to tell you, I didn't look forward to it even though Mom's cooking was incredible. I know the peas stand for luck and tradition. I just couldn't get into it. Those little eyes staring back at you.

So I broke with tradition when left to my own devices. Out of the house, on my own, and with my two boys to raise, I did need a lot of luck. But, still I wasn't tuned into the lucky bean thing. I just took the opportunity to cook what I wanted.

Some years later, I did a segment for one of the local television stations. They wanted black-eyed peas for the occasion. You know, New Year's food. Beans in a pot. Not my thing. So I got a little creative.

I cooked the black-eyed peas and then into a pea mash à la mashed potatoes. I used that as a side with my beloved cabbage casserole. Actually, I put the cabbage casserole on top of the mashed black-eyed peas. I have to say it was a big hit. And, finally, I had something with all the culinary bells and whistles of lucky New Year's Day fare that tastes pretty lucky to me.

Happy New Year's Cabbage Casserole

I found inspiration for this dish in the basic idea of a cabbage soup or cabbage rolls when I became frustrated with an uncooperative head of cabbage with leaves that would tear every time I tried to make a roll. You don't have to be lucky to pull this one off in time for a New Year's feast. **Serves 6 to 8**

---

4 tablespoons unsalted butter

2 cups chopped yellow onion

1 cup chopped celery

1 cup chopped green bell pepper

1/4 cup Creole seasoning

1/2 pound andouille sausage

1 (9 x 13-inch) pan baked sweet cornbread

2 1/2 cups chicken stock

1 head cabbage, roughly chopped

Preheat oven to 350 degrees.

In a large skillet over medium heat, melt butter. Add onions and sauté until translucent, about 5 minutes. Add celery and bell pepper and continue to sauté until vegetables are tender, about 7 minutes. Add Creole seasoning and sausage. Thoroughly mix and continue to heat for 3 minutes. Remove from heat and cool.

In a large mixing bowl, crumble cornbread. Add vegetables mixture and combine. Add stock to moisten, being careful not to make it too soupy. Set aside.

Blanch cabbage in salted water for 10 minutes. Strain off liquid and cool by shocking in an ice-water bath.

In a 9 x 13-inch baking pan, layer cabbage and dressing mixture starting with a layer of cabbage on the bottom about 1/2 inch deep. Finish layering with cabbage on top. Cover tightly with aluminum foil and bake for about 30 minutes. Remove foil and brown for 7 minutes. Remove from oven.

TIPS & SUGGESTIONS

Red cabbage or even a mix of red and green cabbage is a great substitute.

KEVIN'S NOLA NEW YEAR'S CORNED BEEF

The Irish term "corn" or "corning" refers to preserving in a salty brine. Corn is not European but from the Americas, so "corn" actually means a grain and in this case a grain of salt. Thus, salted beef or corned beef. It takes a little bit of planning to get this done, but it is so good and really simple. You should do this at least once in your cooking life. **Serves 8 to 10**

Brine

2 quarts water

1 cup kosher salt

1/2 cup brown sugar

2 tablespoons coriander seeds

1 cinnamon stick

1 tablespoon mustard seeds

1 tablespoon black peppercorns

1 tablespoon fennel seeds

2 teaspoons nutmeg

2 teaspoons celery seeds

8 whole cloves

8 allspice berries

12 juniper berries

8 bay leaves, crumbled

1/2 teaspoon ground ginger

2 pounds ice

1 (5-pound) beef brisket

Brined Brisket

1 yellow onion, quartered

1 large carrot, roughly chopped

1 stalk celery, chopped

Creole mustard

Happy New Year's Cabbage Casserole (facing page)

Brine

In a large stockpot, heat water over medium-high heat. Add salt, brown sugar, and spices and continue to heat until sugar has dissolved. Remove from heat and add ice to cool. Place in refrigerator and cool until about 42–45 degrees.

Trim brisket and place into a 2-gallon ziplock bag. Fill with the chilled brine and cover meat fully. Seal and place into a container in the refrigerator for 10 days to marinate. Check daily to make sure beef remains fully submerged in the brine.

Brined Brisket

After 10 days, remove meat from brine and rinse. Place into a stockpot and add onion, carrot, and celery. Cover with water. Heat on high heat and bring water to a boil. Reduce heat to low, cover, and simmer for 3 hours or until the meat is tender.

Remove from pot and let rest for 15 minutes. Slice across the grain and serve with Creole mustard and cabbage casserole.

TIPS & SUGGESTIONS

You can cook the brined brisket in a pressure cooker to reduce cooking time to 1 1/2 hours at 15 pounds of pressure. Set your calendar for December 20 to start the brining. This way you can be ready for New Year's Day.

BLacK-Eyed Peas and Andouille

For luck, as tradition goes. **Serves 6**

---

6 tablespoons butter

1 cup chopped yellow onion

¹/₂ pound pickled meat

¹/₂ pound andouille sausage

2 tablespoons Creole seasoning

2 tablespoons tomato paste

1 bay leaf

16 ounces dried black-eyed peas, soaked

1 quart chicken stock

Cooked white rice

¹/₄ cup chopped green onions

¹/₄ cup chopped Italian parsley

In a large heavy-bottom soup pan, heat butter and sauté onions until translucent, about 7 minutes. Add pickled meat and andouille. Sauté for 2 minutes. Add Creole seasoning and sauté for about 1 minute. Add tomato paste and bay leaf. Continue to sauté for about 3 minutes to allow flavors to marry. Stir continuously.

Add black-eyed peas and stir for 1 minute. Add stock slowly and continue to stir. Bring to a boil for 1 minute. Reduce heat and simmer for 45 minutes or until beans are tender. Add additional stock if beans become dry. Continue to simmer for another 20 minutes.

Serve over rice and garnish with green onion and parsley.

TIPS & SUGGESTIONS

Soak your beans overnight in the refrigerator for a speedy, tender dish. You can cook this without sausage or try any firm, smoked sausage.

German Heritage

To this day, I'm still fascinated by the pulley system that operated inside Kolb's at 125 St. Charles Avenue, right off of Canal Street. I was always told it was a former stable. I've heard so many stories about Kolb's over the years and always was taken by the atmosphere every time I visited the iconic German restaurant. On the menu were dishes that revolved around cabbage, potatoes, and sausages. German cuisine at its finest in New Orleans. That was my experience as a kid. Big hearty foods, and of course, I was hooked.

German settlers came in droves to New Orleans in the 1800s and left their mark on the city. Many of them migrated to the farmland outside New Orleans and became the main suppliers of produce to the city proper. The Germans were instrumental in creating our food culture for sure. They worked in and around the French Market area where the German ladies selling vegetables were prominent on the scene. As a chef, I believe it is crucial to understand and embrace the contributions of the German settlers to New Orleans.

It's also cool to know that one of the German strongholds outside of New Orleans is called Des Allemands, literally translated "of the Germans." That's where I believe the best fresh water catfish can be found. We do love our catfish here in Louisiana. Thin filets from Des Allemands are the only catfish I want.

In the mid-1990s, I became friends with Chef Bernard Götz, who at the time was the executive chef of the Sheraton Hotel downtown. Back in those days, the big hotels had the good practice of bringing in chefs from around the world. Chef Bernard was a master of creating huge functions and managing large amounts of good, quality food. I was fortunate enough to watch him in action as he showcased New Orleans' culinary traditions to the thousands of conventioneers at the downtown hotel. It was in his kitchen I learned the art of making spaetzle and schnitzel. I am grateful that Chef Bernard taught me that German food is more than cabbage and brats. It's refined and serious like the people that it represents.

Today, German culture, traditions, and the community of those German settlers in New Orleans can be found holding down the fort at the Deutches Haus. The devoted group brings Oktoberfest to New Orleans in a big way. Every year the members recreate the month-long harvest celebration focused around food and music traditions—so very New Orleans.

Beef Rouladen

Rolled meat dishes are common in many cultures and the Rouladen is a perfect example from Germany. This New Orleans version uses mustard with the pickle and is a great tribute to German cuisine and its place in New Orleans' culinary heritage. **Serves 4 to 6**

---

8 strips thick-cut bacon

8 slices beef top round, pounded to $\frac{1}{4}$-inch thickness

Kosher salt and freshly ground pepper, to taste

$\frac{1}{4}$ cup Creole mustard

1 yellow onion, sliced

8 pickle slices (can be spears of sweet pickle or even a garlic pickle)

3 tablespoons vegetable oil

2 cloves garlic, minced

1 cup diced tomatoes

1 cup red wine

$2\frac{1}{2}$ cups beef broth

3 tablespoons all-purpose flour

In a large sauté pan over medium-high heat, cook the bacon enough to render the fat, remove from heat, and set aside.

Prepare the beef by seasoning with salt and pepper and a thin coating of mustard on one side. Place 2 or 3 slices of onion, a pickle slice, and a bacon strip on each slice of beef. Roll and secure with toothpicks or cooking twine.

Return bacon fat to the stovetop and bring to temperature. Brown the Rouladen in the bacon fat on all sides, about 7 minutes. Remove from pan. Add vegetable oil, if needed, and heat. Add remaining onion and sauté until translucent, about 7 minutes. Add garlic and tomatoes and cook until you smell the aroma, about 1 minute. Add wine and deglaze pan, reduce temperature, and add beef broth. Return Rouladen to pan, cover, and reduce heat to a simmer. Cook for about $1\frac{1}{2}$ hours on a simmer until the meat is fork tender. You can turn the Rouladen once halfway through cooking.

Remove Rouladen from pan, turn heat to high, and stir. Add flour to thicken. Season gravy with salt and pepper and serve over Rouladen.

TIPS & Suggestions
You can use any cut of beef pounded to a $\frac{1}{4}$-inch thickness.

POTATO PANCAKES

What kid doesn't like pancakes? Then to take my favorite vegetable and turn it into a pancake—life is good. **Serves 4 to 6**

---

4 large white potatoes

1 egg, beaten

2 teaspoons kosher salt

Freshly ground pepper, to taste

1 yellow onion, chopped

2 tablespoons all-purpose flour

2 tablespoons vegetable oil

Preheat oven to 200 degrees.

Finely grate the potatoes into a large mixing bowl. Drain off any excess liquid.

Whisk together egg, salt, and pepper. Pour over potatoes. Add onion and mix. Sprinkle with flour and continue to mix until you notice a thickening. Place in refrigerator for 15 minutes to chill.

Heat griddle and coat with oil. Divide the potato mixture into ¼-cup portions, place on griddle, and flatten. Fry until golden brown on both sides, about 4 minutes each. Remove and drain on paper towel. Continue with remaining mixture. Hold in oven until ready to serve.

TIPS & SUGGESTIONS

The heartier potatoes work best in this recipe. The smaller, gourmet potatoes are more difficult to shred. Make sure to cook the pancakes through.

RED CABBAGE

Often, when you think of cabbage, you think of it being savory with a delightful twang. The jam in this adds a nice sweet tartness where serving it with meats makes an unexpected pleasure. **Serves 8**

½ pound bacon

1 red onion, sliced

1 red apple, diced

1 head red cabbage, sliced

2 tablespoons red wine vinegar

1 cup dry red wine, divided

½ teaspoon ground cloves

1 bay leaf

2 tablespoons all-purpose flour

2 tablespoons blackberry jam

2 teaspoons sugar

Salt, to taste

In a large skillet on medium-high heat, sauté bacon for 2-3 minutes. Add onion and apples and continue to sauté for 1-2 minutes. Stir in cabbage. Add vinegar, ½ cup wine, cloves, and bay leaf. Cover, reduce heat, and simmer for 45 minutes until cabbage is tender. Sprinkle with flour and stir in jam and sugar. Add the remaining wine and stir. Add salt.

TIPS & SUGGESTIONS

I love to make this and serve with steak from the grill. It's great chilled as a leftover, too. Blueberry jam is also a great choice in place of the blackberry jam.

SHRIMP SPECIALTIES

Mom bought a lot of shrimp from Don's Seafood on Broad Street. Don's was right across the street from the old Bohn Ford, right near the pumping station.

Mom started going there when I was in elementary school. At those times when Uncle Chet didn't bring her what she wanted to cook, or if Dad and I didn't go crabbing, that was her go-to seafood spot close to home. I remember having my first pompano that she bought there. Oysters and crabmeat came from Don's, too. It was the same story. These guys would always show me what was going on behind the scenes. Such a treat for me now looking back.

There was a ritual in the kitchen when it came to seafood that usually involved me, Nan and Mom. I remember many occasions sitting at the table with my Nan, under the strict direction of Mom, peeling shrimp. I learned about the points on the head and tail and was taught how the shrimp protected themselves using their armor. While we chatted, I'd hand off a peeled shrimp to Nan who would butterfly the shrimp with a little paring knife with expert precision. It was a simple pleasure. And, those times were full of fun and love.

My mom cooked the most incredible fried shrimp. The crusty outside was perfectly even and crisped. Her flavor was just the right mix of seasonings and seafood.

I loved it when everyone would keep their shrimp tails to the side. No one in my family ate the tails. As a matter of fact, I believe I just may be a member of an elite group, or as we say in New Orleans, "krewe of connoisseurs" of the crispy shrimp tail. I used to hang out and wait to collect the tails and then continue to devour them with whatever sauce was left over. Yes, I'm the guy that eats the crispy fried tails.

I really enjoy buying the big shrimp called U-12 size for the fact that you get about 12 to a pound. They are just huge and awesome. I remove the head, pull the legs and devein them. I make a filling with soft butter, chopped red bell pepper, and green onion with a dash of salt, I stuff the shrimp at the top and pack it in with a bread crumb topping. You just line them up on a sheet pan and cook for about 8 minutes. Those shells cook off so crunchy and tasty against the soft filling. I've never written out that recipe or really worried about the ratios. I just do it and it's great. It really gives you the full scope of the shrimp, especially knowing that you can pretty much eat the entire thing. Nothing is wasted.

SHRIMP CREOLE

This Creole recipe is a wonderful showcase for our beautiful, locally grown namesake tomatoes. Pair with local poultry or shrimp to create one of New Orleans' signature dishes. Shrimp Creole was originally inspired by the indigenous produce and the influences of the New Orleans cultures that contributed to the birth of this amazing dish. **Serves 4 to 6**

$\frac{1}{2}$ cup butter

$1\frac{1}{2}$ cups chopped onion

1 cup chopped green bell pepper

$\frac{3}{4}$ cup chopped celery

8 cloves garlic, chopped

2 teaspoons salt

$\frac{1}{8}$ teaspoon cayenne pepper

5 tablespoons Creole seasoning, divided

2 bay leaves

32 ounces fresh tomatoes, peeled and seeded, chopped

1 teaspoon Worcestershire sauce

2 teaspoons hot sauce

4 tablespoons water

2 tablespoons all-purpose flour

2 pounds 16/20 shrimp uncooked, headless, peeled, and deveined

$4\frac{1}{2}$ cups cooked white rice

$\frac{1}{3}$ cup chopped green onions

$\frac{1}{4}$ cup chopped Italian parsley

In a large saucepan, melt butter over medium heat. Cook onions until translucent, about 4 minutes, add bell pepper and celery and cook another 3 minutes or until softened. Add garlic and continue to cook until you smell garlic, about 1 minute. Add salt, cayenne, 2 tablespoons Creole seasoning, bay leaves, tomatoes, Worcestershire, and hot sauce. Stir thoroughly and heat to a boil.

Thoroughly combine water with flour, being careful there are not lumps or clumps. Stir into mixture until completely combined and you feel the mixture thickening. Reduce heat and simmer, uncovered, for about 10 minutes.

Season shrimp with remaining seasoning, add to the pan, stir in thoroughly, and bring to a boil.

Reduce heat, cover, and cook until shrimp are pink, about 5 minutes.

Serve over steaming hot rice and garnish with green onion and parsley.

TIPS & SUGGESTIONS

You can add chicken or sausage or even vegetables to create distinctive Creole combinations. I really recommend going as fresh as possible with your ingredients but don't shy away if you have to use canned tomatoes. If you have to go that route, I suggest purchasing very high quality products.

SHRIMP RÉMOULADE

My early memories of shrimp rémoulade were based on my initial perception that the rémoulade sauce would overpower the delicate shrimp. It's just not so. As basic as this dish comes across, its simplistic complexity is a showcase of classic Creole cooking styles. **Serves 4 to 6**

---

2 pounds 16/20 Gulf shrimp, in shell, no heads

1 tablespoon black peppercorns

5 bay leaves

2 large stalks fresh thyme

1 gallon water

3 large lemons, 2 halved and 1 cut into wedges

½ cup Creole Seasoning

1 large head garlic, peeled

1 large onion, cut into chunks

¼ cup kosher salt

Rémoulade sauce, of choice

1 head of lettuce, romaine or iceberg

Rinse shrimp and set aside. Using cheesecloth and kitchen twine, make an herb sachet and fill with peppercorns, bay leaves, and thyme.

In a large stockpot filled with water, add shrimp, sachet, lemon halves, Creole seasoning, garlic, onion, and salt. Bring to a boil. Turn off heat, cover, and let shrimp sit for 5 minutes to absorb flavors. Drain shrimp. Cool and then peel and devein. Leave tails on. Place in refrigerator to chill, about 2 hours.

In a small mixing bowl, toss shrimp in rémoulade. Place a small mound of lettuce on each plate. Top with shrimp and garnish with a lemon wedge.

TIPS & SUGGESTIONS

You can simply serve the rémoulade on the side instead of tossing. Or, you can drizzle the rémoulade. Be creative. It's great either way.

WHITE RÉMOULADE

Makes 2 cups

2 tablespoons white vinegar

2 tablespoons Creole Seasoning

½ cup finely diced green onions

½ cup finely diced celery

2 tablespoons minced garlic

2 teaspoons fresh lemon juice

Salt and pepper, to taste

1½ cups mayonnaise

Combine all ingredients except mayonnaise in a small bowl. Slowly add mayonnaise and stir to fully incorporate. Adjust seasonings.

CLASSIC RICH RED RÉMOULADE

Makes 2 cups

$\frac{1}{3}$ cup extra virgin olive oil

2 tablespoons Creole Seasoning

2 tablespoons paprika

$\frac{1}{8}$ teaspoon cayenne pepper

Salt and pepper, to taste

2 tablespoons red wine

1 tablespoon Worcestershire sauce

$\frac{1}{2}$ cup Creole mustard

$\frac{1}{2}$ cup chopped celery

1/2 cup chopped green onions

$\frac{1}{2}$ cup chopped Italian parsley

Combine oil with Creole seasoning, paprika, cayenne, salt, and pepper; mix thoroughly. Add red wine and Worcestershire and continue to mix. Add Creole mustard and stir. Then finish with celery, onion, and parsley.

TIPS & SUGGESTIONS

The rémoulades are often served chilled. Allowing the rémoulades to chill for a few hours in the fridge really helps the flavor marry. I've also sautéed shrimp and added a few tablespoons to the hot pan and sautéed for a minute or so. Serve that over pasta. The flavors really explode.

New Orleans-Style Barbecue Shrimp

When I first heard of barbecue shrimp, I figured we were firing up the grill. To the amazement of my young mind and healthy appetite, barbecue shrimp gets its classic presentation from the sauce rich with seasonings and butter. The original version is still served today on Napoleon Avenue at Pascal's Manale. They've served this dish since 1913. You can't get anymore New Orleans than that. **Serves 4**

---

2 pounds U-12 Gulf shrimp, head and tail on, unpeeled

12 ounces amber or lager-style beer

3 tablespoons Creole seasoning

$^1/_2$ cup Worcestershire sauce

2 lemons, juiced

$^1/_2$ cup chopped green onions

$^1/_4$ cup chopped Italian parsley

8 cloves garlic, roughly chopped

3 tablespoons freshly cracked pepper

1 cup butter, chilled and cut into cubes

1 loaf French bread, heated

In a large skillet, heat shrimp and beer over medium-high heat until bubbling, about 3 minutes. Add Creole seasoning, Worcestershire, lemon juice, green onion, parsley, garlic, and pepper. Continue to heat until boiling. Reduce heat and simmer for 1 minute. Remove from stovetop. Then stir in butter cubes, whisking quickly to thoroughly incorporate and create a slick sauce. Remove from heat and serve with French bread for dipping.

TIPS & SUGGESTIONS

The classic approach is to cook the shrimp with the heads and tails on and unpeeled. Yep. It's messy. Leaving the shrimp intact adds so much flavor. You can remove the heads and tails and get a similar flavor if you choose. No problem.

EGG DISHES

I eat an egg at least once a day. If you think about it, the egg is the most perfect food. An egg can be a meal on its own. The egg can be used to tie a dish together. A fairly new buzz phrase in the cooking world is "put an egg on it." I couldn't agree more. Whether the dish is sweet or savory, the egg is key.

Grandma Emily made the ultimate soft-boiled egg. I think she just cooked it for three minutes. Truly, I'm not sure exactly what she did. It's one of those things I took for granted and today I truly appreciate. She'd put the finished egg in an egg cup and just crack the top off. She would sprinkle paprika into the egg and then she'd arm you with a spoon. The white was barely cooked and the yolk runny. You'd mix that up and devour it. It just melted in your mouth. I know for certain this is where I began my appreciation for eggs.

New Orleans cuisine has always embraced the egg. With the invention of the classic brunch ritual in New Orleans, eggs became a main focus in cuisine. Not only appearing at breakfast, the Creoles love to pair eggs with all kinds of classic sauces. Brunch in New Orleans just can't happen without the egg.

Eggs Sardou

This recipe is a New Orleans original, and a version of Eggs Benedict, that features creamed spinach and artichoke bottoms. It was invented at Antoine's and made famous as part of the breakfast at Brennan's experience. **Serves 4 to 6**

---

8 Artichoke Bottoms

8 ham slices, ¼ inch thick and pan fried

2 cups Creamed Spinach

8 poached eggs

1 cup hollandaise sauce

6 to 8 boiled shrimp

On each serving plate, start with the Artichoke Bottoms. Top with a slice of ham. Generously layer on the Creamed Spinach. Top each with a poached egg. Finish with hollandaise sauce and garnish with shrimp.

TIPS & SUGGESTIONS

Don't skimp on the hollandaise. I always make extra hollandaise.

ARTICHOKE BOTTOMS

Makes 8

8 artichoke bottoms

8 lemon slices, $\frac{1}{4}$ inch thick

1 teaspoon kosher salt

In a saucepan, place artichoke bottoms in salted water with lemon and warm on low heat until thoroughly heated. Simmer until ready to use, remove with a slotted spoon and drain before placing on the plate.

TIPS & SUGGESTIONS

If you can't find the whole artichoke bottoms, you can use quartered and arrange in a circle. Be sure to use the plain hearts, not the marinated.

CREAMED SPINACH

Makes approximately 2 cups

4 tablespoons unsalted butter

$\frac{1}{4}$ cup all-purpose flour

1 teaspoon white pepper

$\frac{1}{4}$ cup minced onion

2 cups whole milk

Kosher salt, to taste

2 tablespoons minced garlic

10 ounces fresh baby spinach, chopped

$\frac{1}{8}$ teaspoon nutmeg

In a saucepan, melt the butter over medium heat. Add onion and garlic and sauté until cooked, about 5 minutes. Slowly add the flour by sprinkling and whisking continuously to incorporate, being careful to watch the heat and reduce if necessary. You do not want to brown the flour at all. Add the milk and whisk until creamy and the sauce begins to thicken, 2-4 minutes. Stir in spinach and continue to cook until thickened, about 3-4 minutes. Season with pepper, salt, and nutmeg.

TIPS & SUGGESTIONS

You can also use heavy cream or half-and-half for a thicker texture to the creamed spinach.

New Orleans-Style Eggs Benedict

This classic dish is made with English muffins and Canadian bacon—but to make it à la Nouvelle Orleans, we are using toasted French bread and fresh local ham to give it just the right roots for a beautiful New Orleans brunch. Also, I recommend doing what I call the "getting it together in your head" part of making this dish. You need to practice the ballet of timing so all of the ingredients come together in the right order. I've put together the dance that I do when making brunch for friends. **Serves 4 to 8**

This should help you pull your dishes together without a hitch. It goes something like this:

Prepare hollandaise

Prep toast

Prepare boiling water and vinegar

Crack eggs into small ramekin

Start cooking ham

Place toast in oven

Turn ham

Remove from oven and place toast on dish

Layer ham on toast

Poach eggs in water

Remove with slotted spoon and place on top of ham

Top with hollandaise and serve

---

8 fresh ham slices, about ¼ inch thick

Salt and pepper, to taste

8 slices French bread, sliced on the bias

8 eggs

Blender Hollandaise Sauce

Creole seasoning or paprika

In a medium skillet, place ham slices and season with salt and pepper. Cook until heated, about 3 minutes. Turn ham, season, and continue to heat through about 3 minutes. Remove from heat.

Toast French bread slices in oven until crisp, about 3 minutes under the broiler. Arrange on plate and top with ham. Top with poached egg, generously pour over hollandaise sauce, and sprinkle with Creole Seasoning.

Poaching the Perfect Egg

Make no waves—literally. If you drop an egg into rolling, boiling water it will cause the liquids to mix and you'll get a mess. So you want to pay attention to the water and temperature and use the technique to gently lowering the egg into the water. You don't want your water to be boiling. You just want it slowing simmering.

In a small saucepan, bring water and 1 tablespoon of white vinegar to temperature just below boiling, about 210 degrees with a kitchen thermometer or reduce heat slightly when you see tiny bubbles at the bottom of the pan.

To carefully lower the egg, you can use two techniques. You can crack the fresh egg into a ladle and gently lower into the water. For this to work masterfully, you have to have a pan deep enough to lower a ladle. You can also use a small bowl and gently slide out the egg. Use whichever is more convenient and works for you.

Remove egg gently using a slotted spoon when the egg white has formed a creamy white case around the yolk. That's about $1\frac{1}{2}$ minutes. You don't want to overcook. The yolk should remain bright yellow and runny for the Eggs Benedict to be a classic dish marrying the flavors of the egg, ham, and hollandaise.

Blender Hollandaise Sauce

Makes 2 cups

| 6 egg yolks | 2 tablespoons lemon juice | 1 teaspoon kosher salt |
| 1 teaspoon Creole mustard | 1 teaspoon hot sauce or $\frac{1}{8}$ teaspoon cayenne pepper | 1 cup butter, melted |

In a blender, combine eggs, mustard, lemon juice, hot sauce, and salt on a quick pulse, about 5 seconds until blended. Add butter in a slow stream until fully incorporated, about 1 minute.

Keep the sauce warm by placing the blender jar in a hot water bath—bain-marie style. It should hold for about 30 minutes.

Serve warm over egg dishes, grilled meat, or freshly grilled vegetables.

Tips & Suggestions

From the cook's side, Eggs Benedict is all about timing. So read through the recipe and practice in your head. I suggest getting all of the ingredients together and prepare your dish by literally choreographing the steps.

clean-out-the-fridge frittata

Frittata is an Italian word meaning fried and as anyone knows New Orleanians love to fry. And, we love our Italian roots! Of course, we are all about the red gravy—the frittata is a great way to showcase something a bit different that can work as a quick dinner or a great brunch dish.

Basically, the frittata is the Italian version of an omelet . . . and you can easily put this together with leftovers or goodies from the fridge. The frittata is a little easier to make than an omelet in that it remains open faced. You can forget the flip and your guests will flip-out over the results. **Serves 4**

---

1 tablespoon vegetable oil

1 yellow onion, diced

1 yellow bell pepper, chopped

1 green bell pepper, chopped

$^1/_2$ butternut squash, peeled and diced

1 cup chopped broccoli

1 cup thinly sliced mushrooms

2 cloves garlic, chopped

2 tablespoons Creole seasoning

2 teaspoons salt

2 teaspoons freshly cracked pepper

8 large eggs

Preheat oven to 400 degrees.

In a large ovenproof skillet, heat oil and sauté the vegetables. Start with onions and add heartier vegetables first. Cook until vegetables have softened, approximately 5 minutes. Add garlic, Creole seasoning, salt, and pepper. Cook for 1 minute. Remove skillet from heat.

Whisk eggs and add to vegetable mixture. Work eggs over the pan to ensure they are distributed evenly. Return pan to heat and cook for 2 minutes or until you see the edges of the frittata begin to set.

Remove from heat and place in oven. Bake for about 8 minutes or until top of frittata is set. Remove, cool, and slice to serve. Accompany with your favorite spicy sauce.

TIPS & SUGGESTIONS

All you need to worry about is the heat under the pan. Use a low-heat setting. And pay attention to the timing. Cook through time can be anywhere from 5 minutes to 15 minutes. And since you don't need to fold the frittata over like an omelet, you can use a large skillet and even serve directly from the skillet. This is why you finish the frittata in the oven, to keep from burning the bottom.

If you have an electric skillet use it and set it to 225 degrees. You can start and finish the frittata in the skillet. By maintaining the temperature as you can easily do in an electric skillet, the frittata will cook perfectly every time. No need to finish it in the oven after the eggs begin to set, after 4 minutes, just put the lid on it. Continue to cook another 6-8 minutes and it comes out perfectly.

You can try various vegetables and spice combinations. 3 teaspoons oregano, ¼ cup chopped fresh basil, or 3 teaspoons cumin are all good options.

Classic Creole

I'm a Creole descendant and a proud New Orleans chef born in Flint-Goodridge Hospital on Louisiana Avenue. With the help of my mother, I deposited myself into the arms of Dr. Alvin Smith, M.D. Later in life, Dr. Smith would always tell me when we would run into each other that he didn't know what to say to my mother as I slowly made my debut into this world because I was so long and it took me well over 15 minutes once my head peaked out to make my grand entrance. At 6 foot 9 inches tall, I lived up to my reputation.

I consider my Creole heritage a gift and one of the many unique things about me. Creole descendents, like myself, are a gumbo of the rich cultures that came together here in New Orleans.

A classic Creole person is generally understood to be a person with French, Spanish, Native American, and African ancestors in New Orleans. Therefore, I am classic Creole. I embrace my uniqueness full on. I was different growing up and I knew it. It wasn't that we talked about it much. But when you see me, you'll understand. My dad's side is French, Indian, and English. Belton is definitely English. On my mother's side, we are from the French Island of Martinique and Native American as well.

Because of my family's DNA and the unique perspectives from both my mother's Uptown side and my Father's 7th Ward neighborhood, I acquired a total understanding of our New Orleans food culture first hand. Creole food was born in New Orleans and from that fact, mingled with my heritage, I learned a deep appreciation for what is not only my people's food but the food heritage for all of the United States. I really know more now than ever and understand the full perspective of the Creole cooking my grandmothers, Nan and Emily, preserved and passed down to my mother and her to me.

I relish my job where I have the opportunity on a daily basis to share what I learned about food and cooking from the amazing Creole women in my family. It means so much to me to pass along the techniques and recipes they taught me to the thousands of people I reach every year at The New Orleans School of Cooking in the heart of the French Quarter on St. Louis Street.

CRAB AND CORN BISQUE

New Orleanians have access to wonderful, fresh seafood 365 days a year. This bisque recipe highlights crab with sweet, fresh corn. **Serves 6 to 8**

---

4 tablespoons butter

3/4 cup chopped onion

4 cloves garlic, roughly chopped

2 whole bay leaves

3/4 teaspoon cayenne pepper

2 teaspoons Creole seasoning

1 teaspoon freshly ground pepper

4 cups seafood broth, divided

5 ears fresh corn, kernels removed from cobs

3 tablespoons all-purpose flour

1/2 cup whole milk

1/2 cup half-and-half

18 ounces lump crabmeat, fresh picked from shell

1/4 cup chopped green onions

Kosher salt and pepper, to taste

In a large heavy-bottom stockpot, heat butter over medium heat until bubbling but not browned. Add onion and cook until translucent, about 5-7 minutes.

Add garlic, bay leaves, cayenne, Creole seasoning, and pepper. Sauté until you smell the garlic cooking, about 1-2 minutes. Stir continuously. Slowly add 3 3/4 cups broth. Bring to boil and add corn. Reduce heat and simmer for 15 minutes.

Dissolve the flour in the remaining broth, stirring thoroughly to remove all lumps of flour. Add to the milk and mix thoroughly. Place in a blender, combine with half-and-half, and blend for about 30 seconds, until smooth.

Bring the soup heat back to medium and add the milk/flour combination slowly into the simmering soup and stir continuously until the soup begins to noticeably thicken, about 2-3 minutes.

Lower heat to an easy simmer, stir in crabmeat, and cook until warmed, about 3 minutes. Garnish with green onion and season with salt and pepper.

TIP & SUGGESTIONS

If you can't readily purchase fresh crab picked from the shell, you can purchase it canned. Most grocers carry canned pasteurized crabmeat in the refrigerated sections. It works just fine as an option for those far from the shore.

New Orleans Shrimp Étouffée

Étouffée literally means to smother. This roux-based dish is one of the classic dishes of Creole New Orleans. Some people are intimated by the name étouffée because it sounds complicated, but this dish is truly easy to master. And, it has the authentic flavors of New Orleans incorporating both a roux and the trinity. **Serves 6**

½ cup butter

½ cup all-purpose flour

1½ cups chopped onion

¾ cup chopped celery

¾ cup chopped green bell pepper

2 tablespoons Creole seasoning

2 cloves garlic, minced

4 cups shrimp stock

1 cup chopped fresh Creole tomatoes (seeds removed)

3 stalks fresh thyme

3 tablespoons Worcestershire sauce

2 teaspoons hot sauce

3 pounds 16/20 shrimp, peeled and deveined

1 cup chopped green onions

⅛ cup chopped Italian parsley

Kosher salt, to taste

Freshly ground pepper, to taste

Cayenne pepper, to taste

3 cups cooked white Louisiana rice

In a cast iron skillet on medium heat, melt the butter. Stirring constantly with a wooden spoon slowly sprinkle flour, mixing continuously until completely added and about the consistency of wet sand. Continue cooking until roux is the color of peanut butter.

Add the onion, celery, and bell pepper and sauté, adding Creole seasoning and cooking until tender, about 5 minutes. Add the garlic and continue to stir for 1 minute.

Gradually add about ½ cup of the shrimp stock and continuing to stir until the roux and vegetables form a paste, about 1 minute. Add the rest of the stock gradually, stirring to loosen the mixture and fully integrate the flavors. The mixture should have the consistency of a gravy, not too thick, not too thin. Hold back some stock if it appears the sauce is too loose. Bring to a boil and reduce to a simmer.

Add the tomatoes, thyme, Worcestershire, and hot sauce and simmer for 25 minutes.

Add the shrimp and simmer for 5 minutes, or until the shrimp turn bright pink and are cooked through. Stir in green onions and parsley, cover, remove from heat and let sit for 5 minutes. Adjust seasoning with salt, pepper, and cayenne. Serve over rice.

TIPS & SUGGESTIONS

You can make this étouffée recipe with crawfish, chicken, or your favorite vegetables and change the stock for a vegetarian twist.

TRADITIONAL CREOLE LOUISIANA PECAN PRALINE

The original French confection was a simple almond coated in sugar. As New Orleanians are so apt to do, we adapted the classic to suit the available ingredients. The almond was substituted with the pecan, abundant in Louisiana. Cane sugar, and lots of it, cooked down and caramelized with the addition of heavy cream is the classic interpretation of New Orleans' very own candy. When you stop by The New Orleans School of Cooking on St. Louis Street in the heart of the quarter, you can sample one of the best interpretations of the praline in the world. **Makes 24 to 36 pralines**

1¹⁄₂ cups tightly packed light brown sugar

1¹⁄₂ cups sugar

¹⁄₂ cup heavy cream

1 tablespoon Steen's Pure Cane Syrup

3 tablespoons unsalted butter

2 cups Roasted Louisiana Pecans

In a medium heavy-bottom saucepan, combine sugars, cream, syrup, and butter. Bring to a boil over medium heat stirring with a wooden spoon until fully melted, about 10 minutes.

Add pecans carefully and stir to fully coat. Once temperature reaches about 228 degrees, remove from heat and place pan on a protective surface. At this point, the mixture will continue to heat a bit reaching about 235-240 degrees before beginning to cool. Let stand for about 5-10 minutes.

Drop approximately a tablespoon of the mixture at a time onto parchment paper or, if available, a cool marble pastry board, where the pralines will settle into the ubiquitous circular shape.

Let cool and voila! This is the best candy in the world.

ROASTED LOUISIANA PECANS

¹⁄₈ cup butter, melted

3 cups halved pecans

1 teaspoon kosher salt

Preheat oven to 325 degrees. In a small saucepan, melt the butter.

In a large ceramic bowl, add pecans and sprinkle with salt and coat with butter. Spread pecans on an aluminum foil-lined baking sheet. Bake seasoned pecans for approximately 20 minutes or until the pecans are toasted brown. Remove from oven, cool, and store in a dry, sealed container.

TIP & SUGGESTIONS

A candy thermometer is highly suggested, especially for the beginner. Also, be very cautious as the heated sugars can cause quite a burn!

Try different nuts in the praline recipe. Peanuts, macadamia nuts, cashews, pistachios—they are wonderful. And, you can use salted or unsalted or even spicy coated nuts.

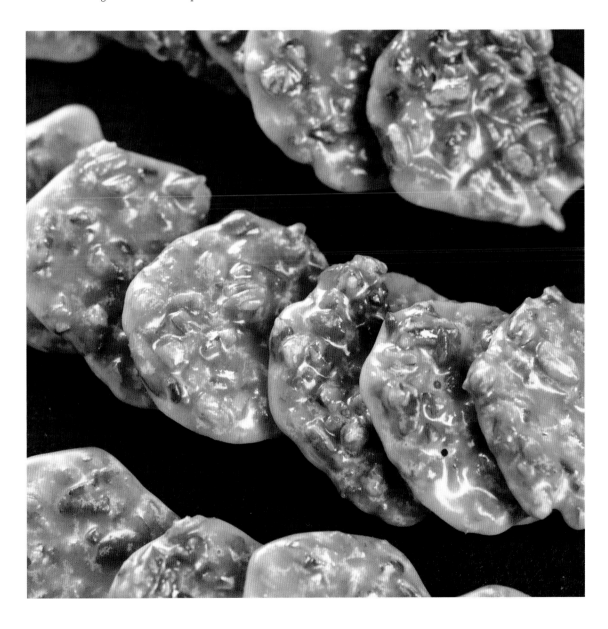

Italian Influences

At Brother Martin High School, I hung out with my buddy Mark Benedetto. And to my good fortune, his family had an authentic Italian restaurant on Tulane Avenue. We'd go over there and his mom would feed us. Benedetto's sat at the corner of S. White and Tulane Avenue right behind the courthouse. It was a tidy little lunch spot, full of courthouse employees and attorneys. This was my first introduction to true Italian food outside of spaghetti and meatballs at home.

In high school, my dear friend Leah Goldman and her family would include me in dinners at Venezia over on Carrollton. It was my first experience with real pizza—the true oven-baked thin crust pie. Mandina's over on Canal in Mid-City is another great place for Italian food. I'm a professed regular. Always our family Italian dinners would end with a visit over to Angelo Brocato's.

This Sicilian family has left an indelible mark as sort of the widely acknowledged king of gelato in New Orleans. It's old school. The handmade cannoli filled with Brocato's proprietary fresh ricotta filling or gelatos are worth the long wait in the hot summer months. I always grab a hand-packed pint of pistachio ice cream to take home.

I started working at The New Orleans School of Cooking beginning in 1991 when our office and teaching lab were located in Jax Brewery. It was then that I had the privilege to get to know the real Quarterites. There was still an abundance of second and third generation Italians active in the Quarter. At the time, I managed the general store and made it a point to keep the olive salad from Central Grocery in stock. That was the time when Sal, Frank, and Larry Tusa were still around every day at Central Grocery knocking out the iconic muffaletta sandwich of which they are credited with inventing. Just two doors down was the Decatur Street location of Perrone & Sons which was a full-on Italian grocery. I would get muffalettas from both Central and Perrone and take 'em over to visiting friends at their hotels as a warm welcome and introduction to just one of the many flavors they were soon to be sampling in the greatest food city in the world.

Years later, Jonathan and Kevin, my sons, and John Perrone's children attended Brother Martin together. Many cultures. Many neighborhoods. There is always a connection. That's New Orleans.

Red Gravy New Orleans Style

It's simply marinara, folks. As you would expect, New Orleanians made a twist on the traditional name. *Makes approximately 2 quarts*

½ cup olive oil

3 cups finely chopped yellow onions

1 head garlic, peeled and sliced

1 teaspoon freshly cracked pepper

1 teaspoon white pepper

3 bay leaves

6 ounces tomato paste

32 ounces cooked tomatoes, peeled, seeded, and puréed

3 cups vegetable stock

2 teaspoons salt

1 teaspoon cayenne pepper

¼ cup finely chopped fresh basil

3 tablespoons chopped fresh oregano

3 tablespoons finely chopped fresh thyme

Heat the oil in a large stockpot. Sauté onions until cooked and translucent, about 10 minutes. Add garlic and continue to sauté for 2 minutes until you smell the aroma. Add the peppers and bay leaves and continue to sauté for 1 minute.

Add tomato paste and stir thoroughly. Cook until the mixture begins to brown, about 2 minutes. Add tomatoes and cook for 1 minute.

Add stock and remaining ingredients. Stir and bring to a boil. Reduce the heat and simmer for 1 hour. Stir occasionally.

TIPS & Suggestions

I don't usually put sugar in my red gravy. Some cooks are accustomed to adding sugar to cut the acidity of the tomatoes. You can add a couple of teaspoons with the tomatoes if you prefer. I usually make this recipe in larger batches so I can freeze half for later.

TRIPLE THREAT MEATBALLS

The combination of the veal, pork, and ground round really is the best way to make authentic Italian meatballs. In New Orleans, we don't just make these for the classic spaghetti and meat-ball dish. These meatballs are the base for an amazing po'boy classic. Meatballs on French bread with red gravy and melted cheese are the building blocks of the ultimate New Orleans meatball po'boy. **Makes about 10 to 12 meatballs**

---

1 large egg, beaten

1/2 cup seasoned breadcrumbs

1/2 cup grated Parmesan cheese

1/4 cup whole milk

1/3 cup chopped Italian parsley

3 cloves garlic, minced

1/4 cup chopped yellow onion

2 teaspoons kosher salt

1 teaspoon freshly ground pepper

1/2 pound ground veal

1/2 pound ground pork

1/2 pound ground round

2 quarts Red Gravy New Orleans Style (page 83)

Preheat oven to 375 degrees.

In a large bowl, combine egg, breadcrumbs, cheese, milk, parsley, garlic, and onion. Mix thoroughly. Add salt and pepper and continue to mix.

Crumble meats to combine, but do so lightly. Add meats to egg mixture and mix well.

Lightly shape mixture into golf ball-size meatballs. Be careful to make the meatballs loosely. If you pack them too tightly, they will become tough. Bake for 20 minutes until cooked to an internal temperature of 160 degrees.

Remove from oven and simmer in red gravy for another 5 minutes.

TIPS & SUGGESTIONS

If you want to limit the meat to only two types, that works just as well. Just add back the volume equally. Pack the meatballs loosely. If the meatballs are packed too tightly they become overworked and tough. A loosely packed meatball will be tender. So try to avoid overworking. Just mix enough to form a loose ball.

TiRAMiSU CUPCAKES

Anytime I go to visit Chef Andrea Apuzzo at Andrea's in Metairie, I always order his tiramisu. I've even gone as far as to order it as an appetizer. It's that good. I owe Chef Andrea a thank you for introducing me to authentic tiramisu and Italian cuisine right here in New Orleans.

Makes about 8 to 10 regular or 4 to 6 extra large cupcakes

CUPCAKES

2 1/2 cups cake flour

2 teaspoons baking powder

1 teaspoon salt

1 cup unsalted butter

1 3/4 cups sugar

3 large eggs plus 1 egg yolk

1 teaspoon vanilla

1/2 cup whole milk

Crushed coffee beans

ESPRESSO SYRUP

1/2 cup water

1/3 cup sugar

2 tablespoons ground espresso

3 tablespoons coffee liqueur

MASCARPONE CREAM

8 ounces mascarpone

1/2 cup powdered sugar

1 1/2 teaspoons vanilla, optional

1 cup heavy cream

CUPCAKES

Preheat oven to 325 degrees. Combine flour, baking powder, and salt in a large bowl.

In a stand mixer, cream the butter and sugar. Slowly add the eggs, making sure to scrape sides of bowl. Add vanilla. Slowly add the flour mixture and milk, alternating between each until fully incorporated and the batter is smooth. Divide evenly into lined cupcake pan. Top with a layer of crushed coffee beans. Bake for 15 minutes until cooked through. Remove from oven and cool.

ESPRESSO SYRUP

In a small saucepan, bring water, sugar, and espresso to a simmer over medium heat until fully incorporated. Remove from heat and add liqueur. Set aside.

MASCARPONE CREAM

Using a stand mixer, cream together mascarpone, sugar, and vanilla; set aside. Whip the cream until soft peaks form, about 5 minutes. Fold cream into mascarpone mixture, a third at a time, lightly mixing to maintain consistency.

Make a deep "X" using a thin knife in the top of each cupcake. Spoon 1 tablespoon of the syrup over each cupcake. Generously frost each cupcake with mascarpone cream.

TIPS & SUGGESTIONS

If making this for a group, use a 9 x 9-inch cake pan. Spread the frosting on the top and cut into squares to serve. Watch the cooking time when using a cake pan. You will need to add a couple of minutes of baking time.

GETTIN' CRABBY

My dad, Oscar Belton, taught me how to crab when I was eight years old. It's really one of the favorite father-son memories from my childhood.

Crabbing starts with a chicken, believe it or not. Dad would have Mom save the chicken necks. The first time he grabbed those chicken necks and these big round nets and said, "Let's go crabbin'," I was like, "What in the world are we going to do?"

He taught me how to tie off the chicken necks in the middle of the net. Then we would throw them out into the middle of the lake (Or what seemed like the middle which was only about 15 feet from the shore. Remember, I was eight!) making sure the rope was secure with the net. And, then maybe we'd fish for 20 minutes. It was like Dad had sonar, because suddenly, and without hesitation, he would start pulling the nets up with just the right precision and tension against the water. Not too fast. Not too slow. Just enough finesse to keep Mr. Crab on the net. Up would come these wonderful blue crabs attached to the net and fighting for the chicken neck. He'd shake them off into an ice chest. The nets would always be filled. Maybe he would toss the net out one more time. All this was done right from the shore. Nothing fancy. Just taking advantage of nature's gift to south Louisiana. Within an hour, you'd have a couple dozen crabs and even a few fish. What an experience!

crab cakes

Everywhere else in the world, people are having salmon croquettes. In New Orleans, we make crab cakes. Creating a crab cake with the perfect balance of meat and breadcrumbs is what we all strive for. **Serves 6**

$^1/_2$ cup butter

$^1/_4$ cup chopped green onions

$^1/_4$ cup chopped green bell pepper

$^1/_4$ cup chopped celery hearts

3 cloves garlic, chopped

3 tablespoons finely chopped parsley

1 teaspoon Worcestershire sauce

2 tablespoons Creole Seasoning

1 cup plus 3 tablespoons seasoned breadcrumbs, divided

$^1/_8$ cup mayonnaise

1 egg, whisked

16 ounces blue crabmeat, picked clean

Salt and pepper, to taste

3 tablespoons vegetable oil

$^1/_2$ cup White Rémoulade (page 66)

Lemon slices

In a large skillet on medium-high heat, melt butter and sauté onions for 2 minutes or until soft. Add bell pepper and celery and continue to sauté for 3 minutes. Add garlic and cook for 1 minute. Remove from heat and set aside to cool.

In a large bowl, combine sautéed vegetables with parsley, Worcestershire, Creole seasoning, 1 cup breadcrumbs, mayonnaise, and egg. Gently add crabmeat, salt, and pepper. Form into patties, dust with remaining breadcrumbs, and chill in refrigerator for 1 hour to set.

Heat vegetable oil over medium heat, sauté crab cakes for about 2 $^1/_2$ minutes each side. Turn gently to avoid crumbling. Serve with rémoulade and garnish with lemon slices.

TIPS & SUGGESTIONS

If you can't get crabmeat for whatever reason, you can blanch a flaky fish like trout, drum, or shrimp, chop, and use it as your main ingredient.

SOFT SHELL CRAB AMANDINE

*From May to July, blue crabs molt their hard winter shell and go through a growing phase. It's at this time that crab-crazy connoisseurs crave the soft-shell crab experience. For people not accustomed to eating soft shells, they are usually converts with the first bite. You get that crunch and you pretty much get to eat the whole crab. It's an amazing food experience especially with a classic amandine preparation. **Serves 4**

---

4 soft shell crabs, cleaned of gills, apron, and eyes

$1/2$ cup all-purpose flour

3 tablespoons Creole seasoning

$1/2$ cup butter

1 egg, whisked

1 teaspoon salt

$1/8$ teaspoon cayenne pepper

$1/2$ cup almond pieces

1 lemon, juiced

2 tablespoons chopped Italian parsley

Lemon wedges

Chill cleaned crabs in refrigerator.

In a shallow bowl large enough to fit the whole crab, combine flour with Creole seasoning.

Melt half of the butter over medium-high heat in a cast iron skillet. When at temperature, coat crabs by dusting with seasoned flour, dipping in egg wash, and again coating in seasoned flour. Place immediately in skillet, top down. Sauté for 2–2$1/2$ minutes or until crabs begin to turn golden brown. Turn and cook the other sides for 2 minutes. Remove, season with salt and cayenne, and set aside.

Add remaining butter and melt. Add almond pieces and stir to coat. Cook until lightly browned, about 2 minutes. Add lemon juice and parsley and cook for another minute. Remove from heat and ladle sauce over warm crabs. Serve with lemon wedges.

TIPS & SUGGESTIONS

You can substitute almonds with pecans or pistachios.

CRABMEAT-STUFFED SHRIMP

I was the official shrimp peeler of the Belton household. Grandma Nan would butterfly the shrimp. Mom made the stuffing. I would watch her make the balls of stuffing and stuff it around the butterflied shrimp, meaning Mom basically wrapped the shrimp in a ball of stuffing. I can best describe them as a crab cake in the form of a shrimp bomb. **Serves 4 to 6**

½ cup butter, divided

¼ cup minced green onions

¼ cup minced green bell pepper

¼ cup minced celery hearts

3 cloves garlic, chopped

3 tablespoons finely chopped parsley

2 teaspoons Worcestershire sauce

2 tablespoons Creole seasoning

1 cup plus 3 tablespoons seasoned breadcrumbs, divided

¼ cup mayonnaise

1 egg, whisked

16 ounces blue crabmeat, picked clean

2 pounds 10/12 shrimp, cleaned, deveined, and butterflied (tails on)

1 lemon, juiced

Salt and pepper, to taste

In a medium skillet on medium-high heat, melt ¼ cup butter and sauté onions for 2 minutes or until soft. Add bell pepper and celery and continue to sauté for 3 minutes. Add garlic and cook for 1 minute. Remove from heat and set aside to cool.

Preheat oven to 350 degrees.

In a large bowl, combine sautéed vegetables with parsley, Worcestershire, Creole seasoning, 1 cup breadcrumbs, mayonnaise, and egg. Add crabmeat and gently hand mix.

Form balls using 2 tablespoons of crab mixture. Press crab mixture balls onto the shrimp and arrange, tails up, in a 9 x 13-inch glass baking dish. Make sure to evenly divide the crab mixture among the shrimp.

Melt remaining butter; add lemon juice and remaining breadcrumbs. Pour over shrimp. Place in oven and bake until done, about 25 minutes. Remove and serve immediately.

TIPS & SUGGESTIONS

If you have any leftovers, reheat in the morning and top with a poached egg and hollandaise sauce. This is a killer breakfast.

TRIO OF SOUPS

Mom made gumbo, chicken noodle soup, vegetable soup, and occasionally a cream soup. Of course, she could make anything, but when it came to soup she certainly had a repertoire. And, when she made soup that was the meal.

I was, and remain, fascinated with New Orleans-style soups. You can count on me to order a soup for my appetizer to this day. I like the diversity and, especially, the subtle changes each chef puts on their soup recipe. In a city where you'll find the prerequisite appetizers on the menus that pretty much are the same from place to place, the soups always tend to be different.

There is something comforting about holding a bowl of warm soup. As a kid, I loved to sneak drinking out of the bowl. It was a great joy when my mom would serve soup in a cup. It was a license to drink it up, served with crispy warm French bread. A good soup makes you smile. Comfort in a bowl.

Crawfish and Corn Bisque

Bisque, a classic French preparation, is part of the Creole cuisine repertoire. New Orleanians enjoy the classic bisque-style soups just as much as gumbo-style soup. The creamed corn in this dish is what really makes a difference. The crawfish combined with the cream makes this dish pop. **Serves 4 to 6**

---

4 tablespoons butter

1/2 cup chopped onion

1/2 cup chopped celery

1/2 cup chopped green bell pepper

2 tablespoons Creole seasoning

1 teaspoon hot sauce

1 teaspoon salt

1 teaspoon freshly cracked pepper

1 1/2 pounds Louisiana crawfish tails

4 ears yellow corn, kernels removed from cob

2 cups Fresh Creamed Corn

2 cups chicken stock

1 pint half-and-half

1/2 cup chopped green onions

In a large skillet on medium-high heat, melt butter. Increase temperature and sauté onion, celery, and bell pepper until onion is translucent, about 5 minutes.

Add Creole seasoning, hot sauce, salt, and pepper. Cook for 1 minute. Add crawfish tails, corn, and stock; stir. Cook for about 5 minutes. Slowly add half-and-half, mixing thoroughly. Simmer for 10 minutes. Season with additional salt and pepper, if desired. Stir in green onion and serve.

Tips & Suggestions

In New Orleans, we always use crawfish in this recipe. But I tell you, this soup is just as good without the crawfish. Shrimp and crab work well if you can't find the tails.

FRESH CREAMED CORN

Makes about 3 cups

5 ears fresh corn	1 tablespoon all-purpose flour	$1/2$ teaspoon pepper
4 tablespoons butter	2 tablespoons water	$1/3$ cup whole milk
$1^1/2$ teaspoons sugar	$1/2$ teaspoon salt	$1/3$ cup half-and-half

Scrape cobs clean of corn into a small bowl, reserving corn kernels and liquid.

In a large skillet over medium-high heat, melt butter; add corn with juices and sugar. Stir and cook until tender, about 5 minutes.

In a small bowl, combine flour and water and mix well to remove lumps. Lower heat to medium; add flour mixture to corn along with salt and pepper. Mix well. Slowly add milk and then slowly add half-and-half, stirring continuously to avoid scalding.

Remove from heat and serve or use immediately.

TIPS & SUGGESTIONS

When fresh corn is out of season, look in the frozen food section for quick frozen, organic corn kernels to use in this recipe.

TURTLE SOUP

Because Uncle Chet went fishing every weekend, the odds were that there would be something extra-ordinary in the cooler besides his limit of redfish or trout. It wasn't unusual for Uncle Chet to hook one of those big and mean Louisiana snapping turtles. I give major props to Uncle Chet for cleaning turtles. It is a big undertaking, but so worth it. The flavors from the meat, which can be dark burgundy in color to a light rosy hue, add depth and character to this New Orleans signature dish. **Serves 6 to 8**

3 pounds turtle meat on the bone or 2 pounds trimmed

1 1/2 cups vegetable oil

1 1/2 cups all-purpose flour

1 cup chopped onion

1/2 cup chopped celery

1/2 cup chopped green bell pepper

4 cloves garlic, peeled and crushed

5 fresh tomatoes, chopped

2 tablespoons Worcestershire sauce

1/2 teaspoon cayenne pepper

1/8 teaspoon allspice

2 teaspoons marjoram

2 tablespoons hot sauce

3 bay leaves

1 tablespoon Creole seasoning

1/4 cup sherry, Almontillado style

8 cups beef broth

1/2 cup chopped parsley

2 tablespoons lemon zest

3 hard boiled eggs, chopped

Kosher salt and freshly cracked pepper, to taste

Juice of 1 lemon

1/2 cup chopped green onions

Heat a large Dutch oven over medium-high heat, brown turtle meat. Remove, cool, and dice. Set aside.

In another large soup pot, heat oil over medium-high heat and gradually add the flour to form a roux. Continue to cook, stirring continuously until the roux becomes a dark-peanut butter color, about 12 minutes.

Add onion and sauté, stirring constantly, until translucent, about 5 minutes. Add celery and bell pepper and continue to cook until vegetables

soften, about 5 minutes. Add garlic and cook until you smell the garlic, about 1 minute. Add the turtle meat and continue to sauté for 1 minute.

Add tomatoes and cook for 1 minute until heated through. Add Worcestershire, cayenne, allspice, marjoram, hot sauce, bay leaves, and Creole seasoning. Stir to fully incorporate and cook for 1 minute.

Add sherry slowly and stir completely. Add broth, 1 cup at a time, until you reach the consistency of a loose gravy. Cover and simmer for 1 hour.

Stir in parsley, lemon zest, and chopped eggs. Season with salt and pepper and then add lemon juice. Garnish with green onion and serve additional sherry on the side.

TIPS & SUGGESTIONS

With a nice bread, I often consider this dish a meal in and of itself. And, truly, beef instead of turtle still gives a fairly authentic experience. I make it both ways and it never fails to be delicious.

oyster and artichoke soup

Most restaurants in New Orleans have this soup on the menu as a starter. We have plenty, plenty of artichokes. This traditional New Orleans soup uses the abundant artichoke, which seems to be the culinary yin to the yang of the oyster. **Serves 4 to 6**

1/2 cup butter

1 cup chopped green onions, divided

1/2 cup chopped celery heart

3 cloves garlic, pressed

5 cups minced fresh artichoke hearts (about 6 to 8 artichokes)

1/4 cup all-purpose flour

1 quart chicken stock

1/3 teaspoon cayenne pepper

1 teaspoon salt

1 tablespoon Worcestershire sauce

1/2 teaspoon fresh thyme

1 quart oysters, drained and chopped (reserve liquor)

1 bay leaf

1/3 cup sherry

3 cups half-and-half

In a heavy-bottom soup pot, melt the butter over medium heat and sauté 1/2 cup green onions for 2 minutes. Add celery and continue to sauté for another 2 minutes. Add garlic and cook until you smell the aroma, about 1 minute. Add the artichokes and sauté to heat through, about 3 minutes.

Sprinkle flour over mixture and continue to stir and coat, being careful not to let the flour brown, about 2 minutes.

Gradually add the stock, stirring constantly. Bring to slow boil. Add the cayenne, salt, Worcestershire, and thyme. Reduce heat and simmer, covered, for 20 minutes.

Add the oyster liquor, bay leaf, and sherry and simmer for 10 minutes. Do not allow the soup to boil. Add the half-and-half and stir to fully incorporate. Add oysters, stirring for an additional 2 minutes. Remove from heat and serve. Garnish with remaining green onions.

TIPS & Suggestions

No matter how long you cook this, absolutely under no circumstances are you to add the oysters until you are ready to eat it. After 2 minutes you are in danger of overcooking the oysters into a hot, mushy mess. It really only takes a minute for oysters to cook through. Just remember that. They cook fast.

DOWN-HOME

I spent my summers in Canton, Mississippi, on the family farm where we grew corn and watermelon. And there was a pretty significant apple and peach orchard behind the homestead, too. Canton is my beautiful Grandmother Nan's stomping grounds. I'm forever grateful for the experiences I gained being a country boy for a few months out of the year.

Canton has a beloved place in my heart. It was for me a cool little town with a traditional town square. When you went from the town square down Union and over to East Academy, you were pointed straight in the direction of my great-grandmother Sarah's house which was next door to my Aunt Doris and Uncle Henry's house which was next door to my Cousins Lennell and Vanessa's house ending at Cousin Scoopy's house. You get the drift. There were a lot of us and everybody farmed all the land behind the houses.

I remember on several occasions under the guidance of my Cousin Ronnie and the baby Anthony walking down the culvert that ran property to property. During the sultry summer months, after the spring rains were done, the dried out pseudo-riverbeds more or less became the chosen path for our ragtag gang.

We'd go to the neighbors and sample the pre-harvest of whatever we could get our hands on, without invitation, I might add. On one particular occasion, pears got the best of us. As usual, Anthony was enlisted to procure the bounty. He harvested what looked like the perfect pears, and we gobbled those pears down as quickly as we could to avoid getting caught. Never mind they were pretty much hard as a rock. It took about 30 minutes, a bit of hot southern sun, and a half mile walk for our bellies to become miniature fermentation tanks. Those rock-hard pears fermented in our stomachs as we trudged back to the house—three extremely sick boys. Not willing to confess, we suffered, and suffered, and suffered. To this day, I know exactly how to check for ripeness of pears, and just about anything else you can squeeze, thump, and smell. Oh, and by the way, never eat a cooking pear!

So Canton summers are about as country as it gets for a city boy from Uptown New Orleans. And, memories of the foods and the cooking at Great-Grandmother Sarah's house stay with me to this day. It's just an unbelievable pedigree I was given. Fresh foods straight from the farm. The meats. The vegetables. The simple and flavorful dishes.

Louisiana Cornbread

Besides French bread, cornbread is served with dishes such as greens or beans because it is like a hearty sponge. It readily absorbs liquid and holds its texture and flavor. My boys, Kevin and Jonathan, used to forgo the rice and crumble cornbread in the bottom of a bowl and spoon their red beans over the top. Cornbread is simply a must for down-home cooking. *Serves 6*

---

2 teaspoons bacon drippings

1 cup coarsely ground yellow cornmeal

1 cup all-purpose flour

1 tablespoon sugar

1 tablespoon baking powder

1/2 teaspoon salt

2 eggs

1 cup half-and-half

4 tablespoons melted butter

1/2 cup pickled jalapeño peppers, sliced and drained

1 cup crumbled cooked bacon

1/2 cup creamed corn

Preheat oven to 425 degrees.

Coat the bottom and sides of an 8-inch cast iron skillet with the bacon grease. Place in oven to heat for 3–5 minutes.

Combine the dry ingredients through a sifter into a large bowl.

In a separate bowl, whisk eggs. Add half-and-half and butter. Combine until smooth. Add to dry ingredients, mixing thoroughly. Add jalapeños, bacon, and creamed corn and stir to incorporate.

Remove hot skillet from oven and slowly pour in batter. Bake for 35 minutes, allowing the top to turn golden brown. Remove and serve with butter.

TIPS & SUGGESTIONS

Making this recipe yields a delicious, basic cornbread that on its own is sweet with a perfect texture. With the addition of the bacon and jalapeños, it becomes a spunky accompaniment.

SMOTHERED GREENS WITH PECAN-SMOKED BACON

Greens are a perfect complement to the spicy, heartiness of ribs. All the ladies in my family, both the city girls and the country girls, were masters of smothered greens. My great-grandmother Sarah, my mother's namesake, had the most perfect greens growing in her Canton garden. As a matter of fact, all my Mississippi aunties and cousins grew spectacular collards within the view of my grandmother's back door. Truly, for a Southern and Creole chef, greens are a quintessential Southern food and complete any down-home meal. **Serves 4 to 6**

---

2 1/2 pounds leafy greens

4 thick-cut slices pecan-smoked bacon cut into 1/2-inch pieces

1/4 cup chopped onion

3 cloves garlic minced

2 teaspoons salt

2 tablespoons sugar

1 teaspoon pepper

Hot sauce, to taste

1/3 cup white vinegar

4 cups chicken stock

Salt and pepper, to taste

Clean greens of thick stems and rinse thoroughly to remove dirt. Tear into small strips by hand.

In a large pot over medium-high heat, cook the bacon until fat is rendered and bacon slices are limp, about 8 minutes. (Reserve 2 teaspoons of bacon fat to use in cornbread recipe.)

Add onion and sauté until translucent, about 3 minutes. Add garlic, salt, sugar, pepper, and hot sauce and continue to cook until garlic aroma is obvious, about 2 minutes. Add vinegar and simmer until mixture reduces, about 5 minutes.

Add the greens and stock and bring to a boil for 1 minute. Reduce the heat and simmer, uncovered, for 25 minutes, until the greens are tender and juicy. If the juices cook out too quickly, add a bit of water. Adjust the seasonings and vinegar, to taste.

TIPS & SUGGESTIONS

Choose collards, mustard greens, or any hearty, leafy green. They all will work. In New Orleans, we often use pickled meat or cubed ham instead of bacon for a traditional flavor.

KEVIN'S DRY AND WET BARBECUE SPARERIBS

My mother went to the trouble to make her ribs the authentic way. Boiling the ribs first to tenderize the meat and then baking the flavors into the meats. To me, there is nothing more down-home than this adaptation of Mom's recipe. **Serves 4 to 6**

---

2 racks pork ribs, trimmed to sections of 3 ribs each

1 tablespoon salt

Chef Kevin's Down-Home Dry Rub

Chef Kevin's Wet Barbecue Sauce

In a large stockpot, bring water to cover, ribs, and salt to a boil. Boil for 10 minutes. Reduce heat and simmer on medium for 20 minutes or until tender. Remove, drain, and pat dry.

Preheat oven to 275 degrees.

Place ribs in a large Dutch oven and season meat with dry rub on both sides. Bake for 10 minutes. Apply a thick coating of barbecue sauce on both sides. Bake for 1 hour. Check and reapply sauce. Continue to bake for 2 more hours. Remove and serve.

TIPS & SUGGESTIONS

If pushed for time, a pressure cooker is a great option. You combine all the ingredients together in the cooker. Once it reaches the proper pressure, it just needs about 13 minutes in the cooker. You can then bake at 325 degrees or grill for 20 minutes. You can substitute beef ribs for the pork and it tastes incredible done with this recipe.

CHEF KEVIN'S DOWN-HOME DRY RUB

Makes about ¾ cup

1 tablespoon kosher salt

½ teaspoon cayenne pepper

2 teaspoons white pepper

1 teaspoon pepper

1 teaspoon cumin

1 teaspoon celery salt

1 tablespoon chili powder

1 tablespoon onion powder

2½ tablespoons garlic powder

1 tablespoon brown sugar

1 tablespoon Creole seasoning

2 tablespoons dry mustard

2 teaspoons allspice

2 teaspoons paprika

Thoroughly combine ingredients. Store in an airtight container for up to a month.

Chef Kevin's Wet Barbecue Sauce

Makes about 2 cups

2 cups ketchup

1/2 cup water

3 tablespoons brown sugar

3 tablespoons sugar

1 tablespoon freshly cracked pepper

2 teaspoons onion powder

1 tablespoon Creole mustard

1 tablespoon white vinegar

2 tablespoons Worcestershire sauce

1 tablespoon Creole seasoning

Thoroughly whisk the seasonings together. Store in an airtight container.

Banana Pudding

Bananas have always been plentiful in New Orleans as our port was the major entry point from Central and South America for the crop entering the United States. Many of the residents of the Bywater, Marigny, French Quarter, and Treme worked unloading the boats at the wharves that lined our riverfront. With such a bounty, it is no surprise that classic desserts made with the banana have always been a sweet staple. Banana pudding is a great way to cool the palate after the spicy, saucy ribs. **Serves 6**

PUDDING

1/3 cup all-purpose flour

1/8 teaspoon salt

2 1/2 cups whole milk

10 ounces sweetened condensed milk

2 egg yolks, lightly whisked

3 teaspoons vanilla

4 cups sliced ripe bananas

4 dozen Nilla Wafers

TOPPING

2 pints heavy whipping cream

1/3 cup powdered sugar

2 teaspoons vanilla

PUDDING

Combine the flour and salt in a small bowl.

In a double boiler over medium heat, warm whole milk. Slowly add flour and whisk to break up any lumps. Stir continuously to fully combine, being careful not to scald milk. Slowly whisk in the condensed milk and yolks. Continue to cook, stirring constantly until thickened, about 8 minutes.

Remove from heat and add vanilla. Let cool for 20 minutes before assembling pudding. While waiting to chill, make the topping.

TOPPING

In a large bowl, beat cream with an electric mixer on medium high. When cream begins to thicken, slowly add sugar, continuing to mix. Once fully thickened, add vanilla and continue to mix for another 30 seconds. Transfer to a nonreactive bowl and refrigerate until ready to serve. This is best served same day.

In a glass baking dish or individual pudding dishes, layer banana slices, wafers, and pudding, alternating layers and ending with pudding. Place in refrigerator and chill for 3 hours. Add topping prior to serving.

TIPS & SUGGESTIONS

This recipe is a great way to use ripe or even overripe fruit. You can create the individual puddings or serve this in one big dish family style.

carnival

The mail doesn't run on Carnival day in New Orleans. That's just an easy example of how things are different for New Orleans on Fat Tuesday. Everywhere else in the United States, it's simply Tuesday, but in New Orleans we celebrate hard. It's a day for fun, friends, family, and food—the four "Fs" of Carnival at the Belton household.

Even though the mail didn't run, Dad went to the Post Office anyway. I just knew when I woke up Dad wouldn't be home. He would always go to the post office early in the morning and sort his mail for the next day. I'd finally get up to the sounds of Mom already cooking. She probably got up with Dad early, early, just to get the gumbo going. The night before she always had the chicken seasoned and ready for frying. And Mom would make her signature potato salad. I'd come into the kitchen with breakfast cooking and Nan would just be hangin' as usual. I knew at some point that my cousins Lorna and Chet would head over to join us for breakfast and then we'd walk over to the parade route. It was the same routine year after year in those early days. And, I'm so grateful that my family and my mom's cooking were always on the menu for Carnival Day.

The cousins would walk over to Napoleon Avenue and catch a glimpse of Rex, the king of Carnival. Catching beads and catching up with friends from the neighborhood was our agenda. Then we'd head back to the house. Nan would be waiting there. Her job on Carnival Day was to man the house. She'd feed you and let you use the bathroom. Anyone who lives in New Orleans, or visits during Carnival, knows that these items are essential during Mardi Gras. Of course, we'd head right back out to St. Charles Avenue to see the truck parades and hang out. As a child, to experience Mardi Gras right in my backyard is just an amazing memory. It was definitely not just another Tuesday.

SHRIMP AND ANDOUILLE GUMBO

People tend to say if you don't have okra in a gumbo then it is not a true gumbo. I say if you do not have a dark roux in your gumbo then you don't have true gumbo. With that being said, just make it like you mean it. It's all good. **Serves 8**

---

1 cup vegetable oil

1 cup all-purpose flour

2 cups chopped onion

1 cup chopped green bell pepper

1 cup chopped celery

3 bay leaves

1½ tablespoons kosher salt

1 tablespoon pepper

3 tablespoons Creole seasoning

1 teaspoon cayenne pepper

6 cups Basic Shrimp Stock

1½ pounds andouille sausage, sliced into ½-inch slices

2 pounds 16/20 shrimp peeled, deveined, and no tails (use tails in stock)

In a large Dutch oven on the stovetop, heat oil. Gradually add flour to form a roux stirring continuously as to not burn. When it reaches the color of chocolate, add onion and cook until transparent, about 5 minutes. Add bell pepper and celery and continue to cook in the roux until softened, about 4 minutes. Stir in the seasonings.

Add the stock slowly. Add the andouille and stir. Bring to a boil and simmer for 30 minutes. Stir in shrimp and continue to simmer for an additional 5-10 minutes.

TIPS & SUGGESTIONS

In New Orleans, andouille is readily available. But in other parts of the world, use your local sausage selections. Kielbasa or chorizo-style sausage works well in gumbo. A firm sausage that holds together is typically the best for gumbo. The classic accompaniment for gumbo is rice. Often, I've substituted potato salad in place of rice, usually just putting a large spoonful right in the center of the gumbo bowl. The potato salad takes the dish to a whole different level.

BASIC SHRIMP STOCK

Makes ½ gallon stock

3 pounds shrimp tails and heads

10 cups water

1 cup roughly chopped onion

2 stalks roughly chopped celery

2 carrots, roughly chopped

3 black peppercorns

2 bay leaves

4 sprigs fresh thyme

½ cup white wine

In a large stockpot, boil shrimp tails and heads in water. Add vegetables and a sachet made with peppercorns, bay leaves, and thyme. Add white wine. Reduce heat and simmer for 3 hours.

Remove from heat and let cool. Strain solids and reserve for cooking.

creole potato salad

Potato salad is often used to complement other dishes during the meal. At home, my family would add it to the gumbo instead of rice. Often, I would make myself a simple potato-salad sandwich. It's two pieces of bread filled with homemade potato salad. Relegating my mother's potato salad to a simple side dish wasn't acceptable to me. Her potato salad was that good.

Serves 8 to 10

---

5 large russet potatoes, cubed and rinsed in cold water

$1/2$ cup finely chopped celery

$1/2$ cup finely chopped green onions

1 tablespoon minced fresh Italian parsley

$1 1/2$ cups New Orleans-style mayonnaise

1 tablespoon yellow mustard

1 tablespoon Creole seasoning

$1/4$ pound bacon, fried crispy and crumbled, optional

Kosher salt and pepper, to taste

In a large pot, boil potatoes until soft, about 20 minutes. Remove from heat, drain, and let cool, about 30 minutes.

Add celery, onion, and parsley and lightly incorporate. Slowly add mayonnaise, starting with $1/2$ cup and incorporate the rest or until you reach the desired consistency. Add mustard, seasoning, and bacon. Mix well but do not overmix. You want the potatoes to hold shape.

Adjust seasoning with salt and pepper. Chill in refrigerator for 2 hours or overnight.

TIPS & SUGGESTIONS

I find russet potatoes are the heartiest and hold together better than other types of potatoes. But any type of potato, like small reds or even fancy fingerlings, is good in this recipe. Even a yam works with the flavors. Mix it up or use what you have available.

12TH NIGHT KING CAKE

Carnival season kicks off on January 6, and so starts King Cake season. For years, the kings of King Cake in New Orleans were places like Manny Randazzo's and Haydel's as well as Gambino's, all local bakeries with amazing reputations. I've had cakes from all of them. When I didn't feel like making King Cake at home, I'd call up and order one delivered to the house. King Cake is forever evolving. The new trend is savory king cakes. But, let's master the sweet version first. **Serves 8 to 10**

KING CAKE

2 envelopes active dry yeast, about 5 teaspoons

1/2 cup sugar

3/4 cup unsalted butter, melted

1 cup warm milk

5 large egg yolks, room temperature

5 cups all-purpose flour

2 teaspoons salt

1 teaspoon freshly grated nutmeg

1 teaspoon allspice

1 teaspoon lemon zest

1 teaspoon vegetable oil

FILLING

1 pound cream cheese, room temperature

1 1/2 cups powdered sugar

1 teaspoon vanilla

KING CAKE ICING

3 tablespoons milk, room temperature

4 cups powdered sugar

3 tablespoons fresh lemon juice

Purple, green, and yellow-gold sugar sprinkles

KING CAKE

Using a stand mixer with a whisk attachment, combine yeast and sugar. Add butter and milk and mix for 1 minute on low speed. Add yolks and continue to mix for 1 minute. Change to a dough hook.

In a separate bowl, combine flour with salt, nutmeg, allspice, and lemon zest. Slowly add flour to egg mixture. Increase speed gradually until dough forms a ball and pulls away from the sides of the bowl, about 3 minutes.

Remove dough from mixer and form a smooth ball. Place in a lightly oiled non-reactive bowl and cover with a towel. Set in a warm, dry place until dough doubles in size, about 2 hours. While it is rising, make the filling.

FILLING

Combine cream cheese, powdered sugar, and vanilla in a large bowl.

Preheat oven to 350 degrees and line a baking sheet with unwaxed parchment paper.

Work the dough on a floured surface into a 30 x 6-inch strand. Fill the inside of the dough with the cream cheese filling. Fold dough over and seal edges to form a long tube. Transfer to the baking sheet and shape into a large ring. You can twist the dough to form an interesting shape. Pinch ends together to form an invisible seam.

Cover with a kitchen towel and place in a warm spot to rise to double in size, about 1 hour.

Bake until golden brown, about 30 minutes, remove from oven and cool.

KING CAKE ICING

In a small mixing bowl, combine milk, powdered sugar, and lemon juice. Blend well. Add more sugar if mixture is too loose.

Ice the cooled cake and sprinkle the colored sugars on in sections.

TIPS & SUGGESTIONS

Add fruit to the cake filling by spreading a thin layer along with the cream cheese. A quick option for the fruit filling addition is buying a prepared jam or jelly. It is a tradition to have a King Cake baby as a surprise. Yes, literally a small effigy of a baby stuck right inside. Be sure to put it inside the cake after baking. The person who receives the slice of cake with the baby is responsible for the next King Cake!

Fresh Catch

My dad went fishing when he had the opportunity and the time. Uncle Chet, on the other hand, made time every weekend to fish. When no one else was catching fish, Uncle Chet would land them. There is a belief that some people have oils in their skin that when they bait the hook just attracts fish. True or not, Uncle Chet had the gift.

Growing up in New Orleans, we were lucky to experience that the fish you ate was swimmin' in the morning and layin' on the plate in the evening. Mom never froze fish, ever. Uncle Chet's gifts appeared regularly. One of his favorite spots was the hot water canal in Michaud. He fished in Lake Pontchartrain. He'd go to Shell Beach and Yscloskey, down in St. Bernard Parish. He probably had secret places we never knew about.

Sometimes we'd get the whole fish scaled and gutted, thanks to Uncle Chet, ready for a coubillion or fresh filet for frying, sautéing, and topping with crabmeat and butter. We had redfish, drum, catfish . . . it didn't matter what it was. My mother made it good. She taught me that when you have fresh seafood as your main ingredient, you don't have to do too much to it. You just want to use your ingredients to compliment, not cover your fresh fish. To this day, I follow her lead.

Pecan-Crusted Redfish

Uncle Chet was Mom's redfish supplier. She'd get her pecans from friends and family, probably from their backyards. We'd sit at the kitchen table cracking shells—my job along with my grandmother Nan's. Nan and I were by far and away Uptown's best kitchen assistants. **Serves 4**

---

4 (6-ounce) redfish filets	1 cup whole milk	1 cup all-purpose flour
2 teaspoons salt	3 cups Italian breadcrumbs	3 tablespoons vegetable oil
2 teaspoons crushed pepper	3 cups crushed roasted pecans	1 tablespoon butter
3 eggs	2 tablespoons Creole seasoning	1 lemon, juiced

Rinse filets and pat dry. Season both sides with salt and pepper.

Make an egg wash by whisking eggs and adding milk. Place in a wide, shallow bowl for dipping filets.

Mix breadcrumbs, pecans, and Creole seasoning in a large bowl. Pulse 2 cups of the mixture at a time in a food processor until finely ground. Place ground mixture in a wide, shallow bowl for dredging. Place flour in a third wide, shallow bowl.

In a cast iron skillet over medium heat, bring oil to temperature. Dip filets in flour, then egg wash and follow with a generous coating of the pecan mixture. Place directly in hot skillet. Cook each side 6–8 minutes, until golden brown. Remove filets and set aside.

In the hot skillet, swirl butter and lemon juice. Cook until butter is melted. Spoon over filets.

Tips & Suggestions

Baking is okay, but will not produce a crispy finished filet. This dish is best fried. You can use other crushed nuts as a substitute for the pecans. Make sure to follow the coating directions exactly. The order is important, dry-wet-dry, as it acts as a glue to keep the nuts crusted to the fish. The breadcrumbs and pecans are listed generously because they will clump as you use them. We made sure you have enough to coat the fish thoroughly. As you master this recipe, you can reduce the breadcrumbs and pecans used for coating.

TROUT MEUNIÈRE

Every time I go to Mandina's on Canal Street, I order the Trout Meunière. At Mandina's, they do a heavier fry on the fish. Mandina's sauce is the pinnacle of the dish. This recipe, for me, is the classic Creole food I love to eat. **Serves 4**

4 (5- to 6-ounce) trout filets

2 teaspoons kosher salt

1 tablespoon Creole seasoning

1 cup all-purpose flour

2 tablespoons olive oil

1/2 cup butter, cut into cubes

1 tablespoon minced shallots

3 tablespoons white wine

1/4 cup fresh lemon juice

2 tablespoons Worcestershire sauce

2 tablespoons plus 1/4 cup chopped Italian parsley, divided

Salt and pepper, to taste

Lemon wedges

Preheat oven to 250 degrees.

Rinse filets and pat dry. Season both sides with kosher salt and Creole seasoning. Dust lightly with flour; set aside.

Heat oil in a large cast iron skillet over medium heat. Sauté filets 3 minutes on each side. Remove to a baking sheet and place in oven to maintain temperature.

Increase heat slightly in skillet. Add butter and melt. Sauté shallots for 1 minute. Add wine, lemon juice, Worcestershire, and 2 tablespoons parsley. Cook for 1 minute. Use a wooden spoon to move ingredients in pan. Season with salt and pepper.

Serve trout with hot Meunière sauce and lemon wedges. Top with remaining parsley.

TIPS & SUGGESTIONS

You can make this dish with other white flaky fish or shrimp. The Worchester sauce adds a depth of flavor to this dish. You can skip it, if you want, but I never do.

THIN-FRIED BEER-BATTERED CATFISH

Farm-raised catfish is more the norm for availability these days. That's why we add the flavors of beer and seasonings. Thin is best, too. When I can get fresh catfish from Des Allemands, it's strictly cornmeal breading without all the extras because that catfish is the best in the world. **Serves 4 to 6**

Peanut oil or vegetable oil*

12 very thin catfish filets

2 cups fine yellow cornmeal or corn flour

1/2 cup all-purpose flour

1 1/2 teaspoons salt

1/8 teaspoon cayenne pepper

16 ounces amber beer

2 tablespoons Creole seasoning

Salt and pepper, to taste

2 tablespoons Italian parsley

Lemon wedges

Sliced red onion

Creole Tartar Sauce

Hot sauce

Preheat deep fryer with oil to 350 degrees. Rinse filets and pat dry. Chill for 15 minutes.

Combine cornmeal, flour, salt, cayenne, and beer to make a batter. Add more liquid as needed. Thoroughly mix to fully incorporate and remove any lumps.

Dip cold filets into batter to thoroughly coat. Immediately place in fryer and fry until golden brown, about 4 minutes. The thin filets will curl in the cooking process, but that is perfect, and the thinness helps achieve the crispiness and flavor profile.

Drain on a paper towel, sprinkle with Creole seasoning, salt, pepper, and parsley, and serve with a lemon wedge, onion slices, and tartar and hot sauces.

*The amount of oil depends if you are using a cast iron skillet, about 2 cups and be prepared to replenish, or a tabletop deep fryer which might require 6 cups or more.

TIPS & SUGGESTIONS

Catfish is a hallmark fish in the heartland of Louisiana. Catfish is always available when the trout and redfish aren't running. Thin filets are my personal preference. And, of course, the catfish from Des Allemands is my favorite.

CREOLE TARTAR SAUCE

1 cup mayonnaise

1 teaspoon Creole mustard

3 tablespoons sweet pickle relish, chopped dill pickle, or dill relish

1 teaspoon lemon juice

Salt and pepper, to taste

Combine all ingredients thoroughly. Refrigerate to chill.

French Beginnings

New Orleans started out French. That was in 1718. And, a lot of water has flowed down the Mississippi River since then. Louisiana was ceded to Spain in 1763. And, then France took it back in 1801. In 1803, Napoleon stepped into the picture and sold us to the United States by way of the Louisiana Purchase.

Obviously, this is a much over-simplified version of history. Luckily, I'm not writing a history discourse, although early in my career, I was a professional tour guide in New Orleans. Interweaved in this back-and-forth between France and Spain is a little lore before all of that, courtesy of our city founder, Bienville, and his encounter with two English ships about nine miles downriver of Jackson Square. Basically, he turned the English ships around by telling them the mouth of the Mississippi River was further west. This is memorialized in an area in New Orleans called English Turn. I can only assume that had this not happened, we would be eating scones and tea instead of beignets and café au lait.

The initial French settlers brought their culture and their traditions. Of the most important were the French cooking techniques. In particular, the mire poix—celery, carrots, and onion, which is the base for all French cooking. But, you couldn't get carrots in Louisiana at the time because they didn't grow in the river silt soil. So the industrious French settlers incorporated the green bell pepper into the Creole mire poix and violà! New Orleans cuisine's distinctive flavor born from the French.

Lemon crème brûlée

*I've been known to squeeze lemon on everything I eat. Lemon along with salt is a natural flavor enhancer. It's no wonder that my favorite dessert would be something made with lemon. In New Orleans, for years there has been something of an unofficial competition for the best crème brûlée in the city. It's on almost every menu and each chef does it a little differently. The crème brûlée is totally French, I might add. I just have to say that Chef Frank Brigtsen at his Uptown namesake restaurant makes the best crème brûlée in New Orleans, in my opinion. I hope my version comes close to paying homage to his brilliant dessert. **Serves 8***

---

1 quart heavy cream

1 cup sugar, divided

5 tablespoons lemon zest

8 large egg yolks

1 vanilla bean, split and scraped

8 teaspoons sugar, divided

1/8 cup powdered sugar

Fresh mint leaves

1 cup fresh berries of choice

In a medium saucepan, bring to a boil cream, 1/2 cup sugar, and lemon zest. Whisk to dissolve the sugar. Reduce heat and simmer for 2 minutes. Remove from heat and set aside.

Whisk the egg yolks, 1/2 cup sugar, and vanilla in a mixing bowl. Slowly whisk in 1 cup of the hot cream. Once incorporated, add this to the remaining hot cream and whisk about 1 minute. Remove from heat and strain. Cool completely.

Preheat oven to 375 degrees.

Fill 8 small ramekins with the cream. Bake in a hot water bath until golden and set, about 50 minutes. Remove from oven and cool. Refrigerate overnight.

Sprinkle tops of each ramekin with about 1 teaspoon sugar. Place under broiler until sugar caramelizes, about 3 minutes. Dust with powdered sugar and garnish with fresh mint and berries.

TIPS & suggestions

I like a very thin coating of sugar for the crème brûlée. The more sugar you coat the tops with, the thicker the candied crust will be. A kitchen torch is sometimes easier to use and achieve consistent results. Just watch closely when you place in the broiler so you don't accidentally burn the tops.

CREOLE DAUBE

*When Mom made a roast, everybody ate it up. You would think that the roast would be my favorite part of this dish. It wasn't at all. It was the vegetables, the gravy, and the herbs that did it for me. This French inspired stew that features root vegetables is the epitome of French-inspired cuisine that stood the test of time in New Orleans. It's not to be confused with Daube Glace, which is a sort of beef in a gelatin mold that is the extension of this dish in New Orleans. **Serves 10 to 12***

---

1 (5-pound) larded roast

1 tablespoon kosher salt

1 tablespoon freshly cracked pepper

3 tablespoons all-purpose flour

3 tablespoons rendered bacon fat

1 shallot, finely chopped

4 ounces tomato paste

2 cups 1/2-inch cubed carrots

2 turnips, cut into 1/2-inch cubes

5 cloves minced garlic

1/4 pound pickled meat, divided into 4 pieces

4 bay leaves

1 bunch fresh thyme, tied as a bouquet

1 cup red wine

4 cups beef stock

Season the roast with salt and pepper. Dust with flour.

Heat the bacon fat in a large Dutch oven on high heat. When hot, sear the roast on all sides until browned, turning throughout the cooking process. Remove the roast.

Add the shallot and reduce the heat to medium. Sauté the shallot and scrape the drippings from the bottom of the pan. Once the shallot begins to brown, add the tomato paste and continue to cook until the paste begins to brown, about 2 minutes. Add carrots, turnips, garlic, pickled meat, bay leaves, and thyme. Deglaze the pan with the wine and increase the heat and boil for about 1 minute. Add stock.

Add stock, return to a boil, and then reduce to a simmer. Simmer, covered tightly, for 4 hours or until roast is tender. Remove roast to cutting board and let rest.

Remove pickled meat, bay leaves, and thyme bundle. Increase heat and reduce sauce by half. Adjust seasoning with salt and pepper.

Slice roast and serve sauce generously over the daube.

LARDED ROAST

5 pound top round roast

1/2 pound pickled meat, trimmed and chopped

1 tablespoon finely chopped Italian parsley

1 tablespoon chopped fresh thyme

4 whole bay leaves, crushed

6 cloves garlic, finely minced

3 tablespoons minced shallot

1/8 teaspoon nutmeg

1/8 teaspoon ground cloves

2 tablespoons kosher salt

1 tablespoon pepper

To season or lard the roast, make 2-inch-deep incisions all over the roast. Set aside. Set pickled meat aside. Thoroughly combine remaining ingredients.

Stuff each incision with the seasoning blend and plug each incision with some pickled meat to hold in place. Place roast in a large non-reactive pan. Cover and chill overnight.

TIPS & SUGGESTIONS

I recommend a top round cut for this recipe. The night before, simply combine the ingredients and "marinate" the roast by coating it with the blend. Follow the procedure and technique to intertwine the meat with the seasoning and throughout the cooking process will yield a more fantastic flavor. It may seem like a lot of work but it is really pretty fun and easy.

spaghetti Bordelaise

Normally you don't think of spaghetti as French at all. Without even having the ingredients in front of me, I can taste the flavors of the garlic, parsley, and wine with butter that are some of the hallmarks of French cooking. I can eat this without any bread or butter or meat—just a fork and a spoon and the Parmesan cheese. **Serves 6 to 8**

---

2 pounds fresh spaghetti

1/4 cup olive oil

10 cloves garlic, minced

1/2 cup chopped green onions

2 teaspoons chopped fresh basil

2 teaspoons chopped oregano

1 teaspoon chopped thyme

1 teaspoon kosher salt

1/2 teaspoon freshly cracked pepper

3 tablespoons dry white wine

3 tablespoons butter

1/3 cup chopped Italian parsley

1/2 cup grated Parmesan cheese

Bring a large stockpot of water to boil over high heat. Cook spaghetti to al dente, remove and drain.

In a large skillet over medium-high heat, bring oil to temperature. Add garlic and sauté for 2 minutes. Add green onions and cook for 2 minutes. Add spices and continue to cook to incorporate flavors, about 2 minutes. Deglaze the pan with the wine and cook for 1 minute. Stir in butter and parsley and cook for another 2-3 minutes.

Toss in the spaghetti and coat thoroughly. Adjust seasoning and serve with grated Parmesan.

TIPS & suggestions

You can pull your pan off the heat and then stir in the butter to make a little thicker sauce. Try it both ways and decide which works best for your palate.

oysters

In the 7th Ward, there was a place called Lavata's. Lavata's was my childhood oyster mecca situated on Claiborne Avenue right near the Circle Food Store by my Grandmother Emily's house, that's Dad's mom. Lavata's was there before they built the I-10 high rise and the Creole neighborhood was intact.

When you walked into the building and stepped onto the white tile floor, you were transported. It was so bright and clean. You might be stepping out of the sunshine, but inside always seemed brighter. On the left, sat a refrigerated counter and people shucking oysters. There were a few tables, and the far right side was lined with tall booths.

As you wound your way through, you'd notice the shuckers popping the oysters into these big glass jars already swimming with oysters in their liquor. They kept those jars chilled in these glass cases. Bags of French bread stood ready. There was a big stove lined with huge cast iron skillets filled with bubbling oil. A cook or two were there with expertise in coating those fresh oysters with cornmeal and popping them into the fryer. This is where I experienced my very first fried oyster po'boy. Thank you, Mom.

Mom would decide when we popped in—usually after we stopped at Mule's (and then Bachemin's after 1969). She didn't announce it or plan for it. We'd be around and then before you knew it, she was leading the way.

Your oyster po'boy came dressed with butter and pickles. That's it. There was ketchup and hot sauce on the tables that you could add, but nothing else. This is as pure as it got.

Lorna's Oyster Patties

This was Aunt Dorothy's go-to appetizer when anyone came over to her house. And, my cousin Lorna's favorite, too. Mom and Aunt Dorothy made the best patties. Bite after bite of oyster goodness. **Serves 4 to 6**

---

4 dozen oysters, chopped and in liquor

1 tablespoon dry white wine

2 tablespoons butter

1 tablespoon all-purpose flour

1/2 cup yellow onion, minced

1/4 cup chopped celery

1/4 cup chopped green bell pepper

3 cloves garlic, chopped

1/2 cup chopped button mushrooms

1/8 cup heavy cream

1 teaspoon salt

1 teaspoon freshly cracked pepper

1/8 teaspoon cayenne pepper

3 tablespoons chopped Italian parsley

1 teaspoon lemon juice

1/4 cup chicken stock

1/4 cup oyster liquor

4 to 6 small pastry shells

Preheat oven to 375 degrees.

In a large saucepan, bring chopped oysters, liquor, and wine to a boil. Reduce heat and simmer for 2 minutes.

In a separate pan, melt butter over medium-high heat. Add flour to make a light roux. Cook for 3 minutes. Add onions and sauté until translucent, about 4 minutes. Add celery and bell pepper and continue to cook until soft, about 3 minutes. Add garlic and sauté for 1 minute. Add mushrooms, cream, salt, pepper, cayenne, parsley, and lemon juice and cook for 2 minutes. Add stock and liquor (as needed) and cook until flavors combine, about 5 minutes. Add oysters and continue to cook for 5 minutes.

Pour filling into pastry shells and bake for 8 minutes or until shells brown.

TIPS & Suggestions

Always use butter for this roux. Fresh parsley is a must, never dried. And, cilantro has a great flavor as a substitute for parsley.

oysters rockefeller

You find this dish on the menu of many, many New Orleans restaurants. It was created by Antoine's owner Jules Alciatore in 1899. Jules was the son of the founder of this more than 150-year-old French Quarter institution. Today, Antoine's still serves this secret recipe. Many a crafty New Orleanian cook has created their own rendition. This is mine. **Serves 6**

---

1 clove garlic

2 cups fresh spinach

1/2 cup chopped green onions

3/4 cup butter, room temperature

1/2 cup Italian breadcrumbs

3 tablespoons anise liqueur

1 teaspoon ground fennel seeds

1 tablespoon hot sauce

1/4 cup chopped Italian parsley

1 teaspoon salt

1 teaspoon pepper

24 fresh and unopened oysters

1 pound rock salt

1/4 cup grated Parmesan cheese

Lemon wedges

Preheat oven to 400 degrees.

Using a food processor, chop garlic. Add spinach and green onions and continue to process using the pulse mode until mixture is finely chopped. Transfer to a small bowl.

Add butter, breadcrumbs, liqueur, fennel, and hot sauce to processor and blend well. Add spinach along with parsley to processor using the pulse mode to loosely blend. Add salt and pepper. Adjust seasoning. Cover and chill.

Shuck and arrange oysters on an ovenproof platter filled with rock salt. Make sure there is at least 1/4 teaspoon of oyster liquor in each shell. Divide the spinach mixture among the oysters. Evenly sprinkle the cheese over each oyster. Bake in the oven until spinach and cheese begins to brown, about 12–15 minutes. Garnish with lemon wedges.

TIPS & suggestions

Instead of spinach, you can make it more in the spirit of the original-style recipe with parsley, celery, and green onions. Also, when using the food processor, I find that I have to add more liquid during the preparation than if I hand chop. If you simply do a hand chop, you will be fine with the amount listed in the recipe.

FRIED OYSTERS AND SPINACH SALAD WITH FRESH PONCHATOULA STRAWBERRIES

I remember the first time I saw Mom batter oysters in cornmeal. Once she fried them, I just couldn't believe how something so soggy and soft became so crispy on the outside and so tender and juicy in the middle. There is nothing that matches that flavor to this day. **Serves 4 to 6**

FRIED OYSTERS

Vegetable oil

2 cups finely ground cornmeal

2 tablespoons Creole seasoning

1 teaspoon salt

1 teaspoon freshly cracked pepper

1 large egg

1/2 cup milk

24 freshly shucked oysters

HERBSAINT DRESSING

1 cup Herbsaint liqueur

3 tablespoons finely diced shallots

2 tablespoons champagne vinegar

1/2 cup mayonnaise

1/2 cup buttermilk

1/2 cup heavy cream

2 tablespoons chopped fresh tarragon

SALAD

1/2 pound thick-cut bacon, cubed

1 pound baby spinach

1 pint Louisiana strawberries, sliced and drained

1 small red onion, thinly sliced

FRIED OYSTERS

Heat deep fryer and oil to 375 degrees.

In a medium bowl, combine cornmeal, Creole seasoning, salt, and pepper. In a separate bowl, whisk egg and milk and season with salt and pepper.

Dip oysters in egg wash. Roll in cornmeal. Dip in egg wash. Right before frying, dip in cornmeal again and immediately place in fryer. Fry until golden brown, about 2 minutes. Drain on paper towel and serve immediately.

HERBSAINT DRESSING

In a small saucepan over medium heat, reduce Herbsaint for 10 minutes or until it reduces to 2 tablespoons. Remove from heat.

In a medium bowl, whisk shallots with vinegar. Let rest for 10 minutes. Whisk in mayonnaise, buttermilk, cream, tarragon, and Herbsaint reduction. Add salt, if necessary. Splash in additional Herbsaint from the bottle to add a bit more punch to dressing.

SALAD

In a sauté pan over medium-high heat, cook bacon until crispy. Drain and set aside.

Arrange spinach on each serving plate. Sprinkle with strawberry slices, red onion, and bacon.

Drizzle with dressing and top with warm fried oysters.

TIP & SUGGESTIONS

Why mess with perfection?

Thanksgiving

The king of the food holidays is definitely Thanksgiving. The Belton's had our family rituals and made the rounds across the city to celebrate. My mom would start cooking the night before. By Thanksgiving morning, the house just smelled incredible. Our house was the place to be at 11:00 a.m. Mom was ready. And I have to say, so was I.

Aunt Dorothy and Uncle Chet, with Lorna and Chet in tow, as well as other relatives would all gather promptly at our house, and Mom was always ready. It is really unbeliev-able what she and Nan pulled off without a glitch. Not one surface in the dining room was empty. Dishes lined the buffet as well as the main table. I remember the gorgeous heavy wooden furniture looking extraordinary. The linen napkins and tablecloth appeared for effect. This was one of a few days out of the year that eating moved from the kitchen and into the formality of the dining room.

One by one, we would fill our plates and pass around the dishes that sometimes would only show up for this special day. I guess Mom was so full from the tasting and fussing that started in the wee hours of the morning, that I really don't remember her eating. But, she made sure everyone else did. These were always incredibly happy times.

When it was time for everyone to depart, Mom packed up food for everyone. And, all this while and through the hustle and bustle, I don't recall there being any dishes to clean at the end of the meal. It seemed effortless. And, because of this, and after cooking all these years, I realize that my mother was truly an extraordinary culinarian.

Late in the afternoon, we would head out to be with Grandma Emily at Uncle Leonard and Aunt Melinda's over in the New Orleans East. Their children, Lisa and Lynette, were like my sisters. Being an only child, it was so terrific that I had these girls from my dad's side of the family.

Thank goodness they ate later in the day. I'd hate to think of what I would have missed out on. I'd walk into that house and it was just sensory overload again. Food was ready to go and filling every surface in the kitchen. We'd grab a plate, fill it up, and head to the den. That was Thanksgiving dinner.

I would take a little bit of everything so I could taste it all. My cousin Lynette, as small as she was and still is to this day, would have more food on her plate than I would. She would clean that plate and an hour and a half later would go make another plate. I have no idea where she put it!

DrY-BrIneD TurKeY

Brining makes a huge difference in the flavor of the turkey. This dry version really simplifies the process if you want to shy away from the liquid brining approach. ***Serves 6 to 8***

---

1 (12-pound) fresh turkey

6 tablespoons kosher salt

6 tablespoons brown sugar

4 tablespoons Creole seasoning

2 1/2 teaspoons ground red pepper

2 teaspoons garlic powder

1/2 cup butter, softened

Rinse turkey and remove giblets. Pat dry with paper towels.

Combine salt, brown sugar, Creole seasoning, red pepper, and garlic powder to create a dry brine. Reserve 2 tablespoons. Take remaining brine and coat turkey inside and out. Cover and refrigerate overnight.

Preheat oven to 425 degrees.

Whip together softened butter and reserved brine. Loosely lifting skin, coat the turkey with the seasoned butter. If necessary, secure skin in place with toothpicks. Tie turkey legs with string and secure wings by tucking into place.

Roast turkey, breast side up, for 45 minutes. Then turn turkey breast side down, reduce oven to 350 degrees, and continue to cook for about 2 1/2 hours or until the thigh reaches 165 degrees. Baste with juices during the cooking time every 30 minutes.

Remove from oven and let stand for 30 minutes before carving.

TIPS & SUGGESTIONS

Make sure your turkey is totally defrosted if you are using a frozen turkey. If you buy your turkey a few days ahead, I suggest brining for a couple of days. The longer you brine, the better the results.

STUFFED MIRLITON

Mr. Valtau, who was a postman with my dad, used to give us mirliton off his backyard plant. Mom would boil them and remove the seed. I just didn't understand why the fuss, because on its own, it didn't really have any flavor. Once she worked her magic and filled those empty mirliton shells, you would have a creation so uniquely New Orleans. There is even a festival celebrating this vegetable. It's just an amazing vehicle for other flavors, and by virtue, is able to reflect it subtleness by marrying so perfectly with seafood or other seasonings. I really have to give it to my momma for being the master of the mirliton. **Serves 4 to 6**

---

4 whole mirlitons

$^3/_4$ pound medium Gulf shrimp, peeled and deveined

1 tablespoon Creole seasoning, divided

4 tablespoons butter

$^1/_2$ cup chopped onion

$^1/_4$ cup chopped celery

$^1/_4$ cup chopped green bell pepper

1 tablespoon chopped garlic

1 teaspoon salt

1 teaspoon pepper

$^1/_2$ pound fresh crabmeat

$^1/_2$ cup seasoned Italian breadcrumbs

In a large soup pot, bring mirlitons to a boil and boil until you can slice without getting them over-cooked, about 20 minutes. Remove from heat, drain, and cool.

Chop the shrimp and place in a nonreactive bowl. Season with half the Creole seasoning, cover, and refrigerate until ready to use.

Remove seeds from the mirlitons. Scoop out pulp, removing as much as possible, leaving about $^1/_4$ inch to make a shell with just enough flesh inside to hold form. Reserve pulp.

Preheat oven to 350 degrees.

Melt butter in a large sauté pan and sauté onion, celery, and bell pepper until tender, about 5 minutes. Add garlic and cook 1 minute. Add mirliton

pulp. Sprinkle with remaining Creole seasoning, salt, and pepper. Cook for 8-10 minutes on very low heat to marry flavors. Add shrimp and crab-meat and cook for 6 minutes. Adjust seasoning.

Season inside of mirliton shells with salt and pepper and place on a baking sheet. Fill mirlitons with stuffing and top with breadcrumbs. Bake for 20-25 minutes or until breadcrumbs brown.

TIPS & SUGGESTIONS

The mirliton is known by many different names such as chayote, christophene, and cho-cho as well as many, many others and is grown in many countries. It looks like a wrinkly pear with a pair of lips at the bottom.

DIRTY RICE

Not literally, but what we mean by this is dirty with flavor. My mom would kill it with the dirty rice. I was, and remain to this day, in awe of how she used everything she bought. This recipe is a great way to use that little packet of what we call "awfuls"—the insides of the turkey. In other parts of the world, you get giblet gravy. Forget that and bring on the Dirty Rice. **Serves 6**

---

2 tablespoons vegetable oil

1 pound ground pork sausage

1/2 pound chicken livers

1 small onion, finely chopped

1/4 cup finely chopped celery

1/4 cup finely chopped green bell pepper

4 cloves garlic, chopped

1 1/2 teaspoons salt

1 teaspoon pepper

1 teaspoon chili powder

1 tablespoon dried oregano

1 1/2 cups chicken broth, divided

3 cups cooked long-grain rice

1/2 cup chopped green onions

In a large sauté pan, heat oil over medium-high heat and add the pork and livers. Sauté until browned, about 10 minutes. Add vegetables and sauté until browned, about 10 minutes. Add garlic, salt, pepper, chili powder, and oregano and stir. Allow the mixture to continue to cook and the meat to stick to the bottom of the pan, about 5 minutes.

Deglaze the pan with 1/4 cup of the broth and cook down, about 10 minutes.

Add rice, remaining broth, and green onions. Continue to cook until the liquid is absorbed, about 15 minutes.

TIPS & SUGGESTIONS

If you want to sauté the livers and sausage first then add cooked rice, it's a little quicker. But really the best flavor comes from cooking the rice with the meats and seasonings.

LOUISIANA PECAN PIE

Our pecan harvest came from Aunt Dorothy and Uncle Chet's backyard over in the Carrollton neighborhood. Most of our friends and family had pecan trees, too. It was a normal thing for us around October to sit in the kitchen and shell pecans. **Serves 6**

1 (9-inch) deep-dish pie crust

1 1/2 cups pecan halves

4 eggs

1/2 teaspoon salt

3/4 cup light corn syrup

3/4 cup Steen's Pure Cane Syrup

1 teaspoon vanilla

1/3 cup butter, melted

Preheat oven to 350 degrees and fill pie crust with pecans. Set aside.

Beat eggs with a mixer until foamy, about 1 minute.

Cream together salt, syrups, vanilla, and butter. Pour into egg mixture. Pour over pecans and bake for 45 minutes.

TIPS & SUGGESTIONS

You can use other types of nuts. And, if you can't find Louisiana's own Steen's Pure Cane Syrup, you can substitute any dark corn syrup.

Wash Day

Sunday was family day, and after a weekend, many ladies took Monday to get the wash done. Getting clothing and household items washed was an all-day undertaking and very labor intensive. My great-grandmother had an old-school washing machine—the kind of machine that washed the clothes in a large metal drum and you had to feed the clothes through what looked like two rolling pins that would squeeze the excess water out of the clean clothes. I remember her doing laundry for hours on end and periodically checking her pot of beans. Since getting the laundry done was the priority on Monday, a meal was needed that you did not have to continually attend. Red Beans and Rice was the answer. This was also a great way to use a hambone leftover from Sunday dinner. Because of this, Red Beans and Rice on Monday is a New Orleans tradition.

The tradition of Monday red beans was adjusted for the modern times I grew up in. My mother was a working mother. One of the things I loved about her red beans is that she always added a fried pork chop or even fried chicken to go with the beans. Paneed meat was also a wonderful addition. So we got the beans on Monday but not the laundry, thank goodness. Mom did the wash on Saturday. She was a full-time teacher at Straight Business School during the week, so Monday was out of the question for heavy tasks.

She taught English, shorthand, and typing. The students loved her. And, she was very good at what she did. I remember every summer she would take a poster board and draw the typewriter keys on the poster board. I would sit in my room and practice typing. I can still hear her call up the stairs, "Kevin are you hitting the keys?" Which I would reply, "Yes, Mom." Ironically, to this day, I cannot type. Thank goodness the cooking stuck.

paneed veal

When Mom bought the thin veal slices from Mr. Walter, the butcher on St. Bernard, I knew that she would take these thin cutlets and "pane" them, which means simply to pan fry. That platter would be piled high, and I couldn't focus on anything else but the smell and the taste.

Serves 4

---

6 veal cutlets

2 tablespoons Creole seasoning

2 eggs

2 tablespoons whole milk

1¹⁄₂ cups seasoned Italian breadcrumbs

¹⁄₂ cup vegetable oil

1 cup all-purpose flour

Wrap each cutlet in plastic and pound very thin. Thoroughly season each cutlet with Creole seasoning.

Make an egg wash with eggs and milk in a flat bowl. Place breadcrumbs in separate bowl.

Heat the oil in a large cast iron skillet over medium-high heat.

Pane the cutlets by dusting with flour, coating with the egg wash, then coating with the breadcrumbs. Place directly in skillet and fry the cutlets on each side for about 40 seconds. Remove and drain on a paper towel.

TIPS & Suggestions

Make sure the cutlets are thin. No more than ¹⁄₄ inch thick. They cook very quickly. You just want them nice and golden brown on each side. Add them to a bowl of red beans and rice. It's amazing.

Red Beans and Rice

Because Mom taught full-time, she cooked our red beans on Saturday and kept them for Monday dinner. She would always add a paneed meat or fried pork chop and that would be dinner every Monday.

As I got older, I became friends with a gentleman named Buster Holmes, a longshoreman, who opened a restaurant on Burgundy Street in the French Quarter. His specialty was red beans. You could get your Monday fix at Mr. Buster's any day of the week. **Serves 4 to 6**

---

2 tablespoons vegetable oil

1 medium yellow onion, chopped

1/2 cup chopped celery

6 cloves garlic

2 tablespoons Creole seasoning

1 teaspoon hot sauce

1/8 teaspoon cayenne pepper

1 pound pickled meat

2 bay leaves

2 1/2 quarts chicken stock

1 pound red beans, sorted and soaked overnight

2 teaspoons kosher salt

1 teaspoon pepper

3 cups cooked rice

1/2 cup chopped green onions

Heat oil in a large soup pot over medium-high heat. Add onion and celery. Sauté until onion is translucent and celery is soft, about 8 minutes. Add garlic and sauté 1 minute.

Add Creole seasoning, hot sauce, and cayenne. Mix and continue to cook for 1 minute. Add pickled meat and bay leaves and sauté for 1 minute.

Add stock and beans and stir until it boils, about 8 minutes. Add salt and pepper and reduce heat to simmer; cover and cook for 1 1/2 hours. Check pot every 20 minutes and stir to incorporate flavors.

Uncover and continue to simmer for another 30 minutes. If you need to thicken up the pot, use a potato masher to mash some of the beans. Serve over rice and garnish with green onions.

TIPS & Suggestions

Grandmother Nan said you have to soak the beans. Soaking is what makes the red beans turn out that creamy consistency that is just so indicative of the New Orleans dish.

Bread Pudding with Whiskey Sauce

Grandmother only made raisin bread pudding. The nuns at Our Lady of Lourdes only made raisin bread pudding all year long. I have created 28 versions of bread pudding that do not include raisins. But to prove I can do it, and make it good, here it is! **Serves 4 to 6**

2 cups sugar

5 large eggs, beaten

2 cups milk

2 teaspoons vanilla

1 teaspoon ground cinnamon

3 cups cubed stale French bread

1/2 cup packed brown sugar

4 tablespoons butter

1/2 cup chopped pecans

1 cup raisins

Preheat oven to 350 degrees and grease a 9 x 12-inch baking dish.

In a large nonreactive bowl, combine sugar, eggs, and milk. Add vanilla and cinnamon. Add bread cubes and allow to marinate for about 20 minutes.

Combine brown sugar with butter and pecans and set aside.

Add raisins to the bread mixture. Stir to incorporate. Pour bread mixture into baking dish. Top with brown sugar mix. Bake for 30 minutes or until cooked through.

TIPS & Suggestions

Put your bread in a paper bag to make sure it dries out for approximately for 3-4 days. If you are using a dense loaf of bread, you may slice it before placing it in the paper bag to help it dry out thoroughly. This helps the bread uniformly absorb the custard mixture, and just makes for a better dish. You can also add semisweet chocolate morsels, to taste, when you add in the raisins.

Whiskey Sauce

8 tablespoons butter

1 cup powdered sugar

1 egg, beaten

2 ounces whiskey

In a small saucepan over a low heat, melt butter and add sugar. Whisk until mixture is completely combined. Whisk in egg then take pan off the heat. Stir in whiskey. Pour over bread pudding.

TIPS & Suggestions

You can substitute milk, lemon, lime, or orange juice, or even water in place of the whiskey.

Garden Harvest

We didn't go to the grocery store for our vegetables. And, we didn't grow them, either. My mother and grandmother bought them off the back of the truck, literally.

The neighborhood vegetable truck wasn't just any old truck. It was a rolling vegetable garden full of the day's harvest from local farms. It wasn't scheduled at any certain time. But households in New Orleans were tuned in and turned on to the fact that when you heard the call, you jumped up and headed to the street for what amounts to V.I.P. delivery.

Our vegetable truck had a wooden canopy built over the back of the truck bed. The tailgate was down and balancing a scale on the back. Piled high under the canopy and perfectly balanced were produce crates filled with colorful fruits and vegetables. The colors were glossy and vibrant.

A couple of times a week, Saturday for sure, you'd hear a booming voice over a makeshift bullhorn rig calling out, "Hey lady, I got 'cha mustard greens. I got 'cha collard greens. Got 'cha mirliton. I got bananas, pears, and apples." It was like a little song.

I remember my mother would say, "Kevin, go get my purse." And, out the door and down to the street she would go so she could catch him. I brought the whole purse, never just the wallet. By the time I made it out, she'd picked out everything we needed. What a way to shop.

If you missed the truck, there were certain spots in the city where the vegetable vendors would set up. There was one in every neighborhood. You could also find amazing vegetables in the French Market.

Today, I still buy fruits and vegetables from the streets of New Orleans. Mr. Okra has continued the tradition of neighborhood produce trucks. He sings the songs and sells amazing produce the old-fashioned New Orleans neighborhood way.

I also buy my fruits and vegetables in the French Quarter from Clarence. He is a unique hybrid of the vegetable truck. Clarence works on foot carrying a few boxes of produce with him. You can guarantee that at least once a day, sometimes more, he'll pass by carrying a crate of whatever is seasonal. Literally, I just reach in and buy right out of the box. It's amazing that he keeps this tradition alive.

corn and sweet pepper relish

This recipe features one of our favorite vegetables in New Orleans, the bell pepper. I keep pints of the relish in the pantry to pop open as an accompaniment to fried catfish, fried chicken, and salads. Also, I sneak a little with crackers. It really is like a Louisiana salsa. **Makes about 9 (1-pint) jars**

---

12 to 16 ears fresh corn, husked and silks removed

2 1/2 cups diced red bell pepper

2 1/2 cups diced green bell pepper

2 1/2 cups chopped celery

1 1/4 cups chopped white onion

1 3/4 cups white sugar

5 cups Steen's Pure Cane Vinegar (5% or a light vinegar)

2 1/2 tablespoons kosher salt

2 1/2 teaspoons celery seed

2 1/2 tablespoons dry mustard

1 1/4 teaspoons ground turmeric

9 sterilized 1-pint jars

In a large stockpot, blanch corn in boiling water for 5 minutes. Remove and shock in an ice bath. Drain and remove kernels from cob being careful not to scrape and produce excess juice; set aside.

In a large pot, combine peppers, celery, onions, sugar, vinegar, salt, and celery seed. Cover pan and heat on medium-high heat. Bring to a boil, remove cover, and boil for 5 minutes, stirring occasionally.

In a small bowl, mix mustard and turmeric. Using a little bit of the liquid from the pepper boil, make a paste of the mustard and turmeric. Add the seasoning to the vegetables along with the corn. Stir and return to a boil.

Remove from heat and pack it loosely while boiling hot into pint jars. Follow your pressure canner directions to finish preserving the relish.

TIPS & SUGGESTIONS

Be sure to make a paste out the turmeric and mustard before adding. The paste keeps these seasonings from lumping when added to the vegetables. The relish can be thickened by adding an all-purpose flour/water blend. Use 1/4 cup of flour in 1/4 cup of water and mix to remove lumps. When you add to the vegetable mixture, you must stir to keep it from scorching. Carefully prepare the pint jars and lids by following accepted sterilization standards. I use the Presto pressure canner and strictly follow their directions.

creole okra

I remember the first time I became aware of okra. I was standing in Schwegmann's Grocery holding a little green spear and snapping the tip. My mother taught me that this was how you knew the okra was fresh. I always wondered how something that looked so furry and green and tough could taste so amazing. Of course, that slimy texture is perfect for thickening gumbo, which is mostly what people think of when you start talking about okra. For me, it's different. The ladies in my family made it as a side dish or smothered it with tomatoes. It's great fried as well. The options for okra are endless. **Serves 4**

---

2 tablespoons vegetable oil or butter

1 cup chopped onion

1/4 cup chopped green bell pepper

4 cloves garlic, chopped

2 tablespoons Creole seasoning

1 pound fresh tomatoes, chopped

2 sprigs fresh thyme

1/8 teaspoon cayenne pepper

1 pound Louisiana okra, sliced into 1/4-inch rounds, caps included

1/2 cup vegetable broth

1 tablespoon vinegar

Salt and pepper, to taste

In a large skillet, heat oil over medium heat and sauté onion until translucent, about 5 minutes. Add bell pepper and cook until limp, about 2 minutes. Add garlic and cook for 1 minute. Add Creole seasoning, stir, and cook for 1 minute. Add tomatoes and heat through, about 2 minutes. Add thyme and cayenne and stir. Simmer for 5 minutes.

Add okra and stir. Add broth and vinegar, cover, and simmer for 15-20 minutes or until okra has cooked. Okra will begin to get slimy in about 5 minutes. Continue to cook through until slime is reduced. Season with salt and pepper.

TIPS & Suggestions

If you choose to use frozen okra, it's not as slimy. You can add it right into your cooking pot. I still prefer fresh okra. I believe in using it fresh, even though you have to cook it longer to get past the slimy stage, so you get all of the flavors and richness from the vegetable.

Fried Green Tomatoes

Tomatoes in South Louisiana are simply special. The flavor from a Creole tomato is unparalleled. You might not have a full-on garden, but most households have a couple of plants in pots on the front or back porch. This dish came about when you just couldn't wait for the tomatoes to ripen. It's the firmness of the green tomato and its edgy tang before the flavors are fully developed that make this an unexpected perfection. **Serves 6 to 8**

Vegetable oil

4 large green tomatoes, sliced into ¼-inch-thick slices and chilled

1 teaspoon kosher salt

1 teaspoon freshly cracked pepper

1 cup all-purpose flour

1 tablespoon Creole seasoning

2 eggs, whisked

2 tablespoons buttermilk

Salt and pepper, to taste

1 cup Italian breadcrumbs or fine cornmeal

Preheat oil (¼ inch deep so as not to cover tomatoes with grease) in a 10-inch skillet to 375 degrees.

Season tomatoes on both sides with 1 teaspoon salt and 1 teaspoon pepper.

In a small bowl, combine flour and Creole seasoning. In another bowl, whisk eggs and buttermilk. Season with salt and pepper. And, in another bowl, have breadcrumbs ready for dipping.

To coat, dip tomatoes in flour, then egg mixture, and finally in breadcrumbs. Fry a few slices at a time to not overcrowd the skillet. Cook about 2½ minutes. Drain slices on paper towels. Season the crispy tomatoes with additional salt, if needed.

TIPS & SUGGESTIONS

Make sure you slice the tomatoes at least ¼ inch thick. Combine with the Shrimp Rémoulade recipe (page 66) and you have a real meal.

POTATOES

There is just something about a Louisiana sweet potato. Some people call them yams. But call them what you want, they are simply good. They are part of my culinary repertoire, always. I've been eating them all of my life. Cook me sweet potatoes any kind of way. It really doesn't matter to me. I never met a potato I didn't like. Maybe I'm part Irish.

It's funny that Mom and Grandma Emily always had potatoes so many different ways. From potato salad and candied yams to potatoes au gratin and, of course, Mom's homemade French fries. Grandma Emily would make an amazing potato soup. The potato can become so many things in the culinary world from a starter and a side dish to a main course.

I loved helping Nan peel potatoes. While she sat watching over the kitchen, she'd peel. I remember being given a peeler at age seven and learned to peel away. I felt very important given this serious task.

Mom would make candied yams. I remember seeing these orange-glazed coated discs of goodness. I have tried so many different ways to cook them and to no avail—they have never come out as amazing as Mom's. I remember her doing butter, sugar, and a little bit of milk. All of the sudden, they were shiny and glazed with a thick syrup. She'd serve them with turkey, chicken, or roast. We had them throughout the year, not just during the holidays.

SWEET POTATO GNOCCHI WITH SAGE AND FETA

I love adding this Italian twist to the Louisiana sweet potato. It's a great recipe for adding that little sweetness to your side dish. **Serves 6**

---

2 pounds Louisiana sweet potatoes, cleaned and patted dry

12 ounces fresh ricotta cheese, drained

1 cup finely grated Parmesan cheese

1 tablespoon Steen's Pure Cane Syrup

2 tablespoons salt, divided

1 teaspoon freshly grated nutmeg

1 teaspoon ground allspice

2 1/2 cups all-purpose flour

1 cup butter

1/2 cup fresh sage

Salt and pepper, to taste

1/2 cup crumbled feta cheese

Preheat oven to 375 degrees.

Pierce sweet potatoes all over with a fork and bake potatoes in skin until soft, about 45 minutes. Remove from oven and cool completely. When cooled, cut in half and remove flesh and discard skins.

In a large bowl, mash 3 cups of cooked sweet potato. Add ricotta cheese and blend thoroughly. Add Parmesan, Steen's, 1 tablespoon salt, nutmeg, and allspice. Mash together thoroughly. Slowly mix in flour to form dough.

On a floured surface, divide dough into 6 sections. Using your palms (liberally dust with flour), form each piece into a long rope about 1 inch wide and 20 inches long. Continue to sprinkle with flour if dough rope becomes sticky. Cut each rope into 20 pieces. Do a little mash on the gnocchi with a fork. Place on baking sheet.

Bring a large pot of water to a boil with 1 tablespoon salt. Boil 20 gnocchi at a time until tender, about 5 minutes. Remove with a dipping colander, drain, and hold on a baking sheet.

Preheat oven to 300 degrees.

In a large sauté pan, melt butter over medium high heat and cook until butter is browned and gives off a nutty aroma, about 5 minutes. Add sage, salt, and pepper.

In a skillet, sauté small batches of gnocchi in browned butter to heat through, about 5 minutes. Hold gnocchi in oven until all are cooked. Divide into bowls and sprinkle with feta cheese.

TIPS & SUGGESTIONS

It's just as good without the feta. Chopped pecans are also a tasty addition for a garnish. The pecans add a little crunch.

sweet potato pecan casserole

I'm a fan of sweet and savory. So I love making side dishes that feature the sweetness that compliments the savory. The little crunch of pecans on top adds the texture that completes this dish for me. **Serves 6**

2 pounds sweet potatoes, peeled and boiled to yield 3 cups mashed

1 teaspoon nutmeg

1 teaspoon allspice

1 teaspoon cinnamon

1 teaspoon vanilla

½ cup melted butter

⅓ cup whole milk

¾ cup sugar

2 eggs beaten

⅛ teaspoon salt

5 tablespoons melted butter

¾ cup brown sugar

¾ cup all-purpose flour

1 cup pecan pieces

Preheat oven to 350 degrees.

Combine sweet potatoes, nutmeg, allspice, cinnamon, and vanilla in a large bowl. Mix in ½ cup butter, milk, sugar, and eggs. Add salt and stir until fully mixed. Pour into a 10-inch cast iron skillet.

In a separate bowl, combine 5 tablespoons melted butter with brown sugar, flour, and pecan pieces to make a crumble. Generously top sweet potato mash with crumble and bake for 30 minutes until top is golden brown. Remove from oven and let rest for 20 minutes before serving, giving casserole time to solidify.

TIPS & suggestions

A sprinkle of coconut to the top while baking adds another dimension to this dish. You can use already spiced canned sweet potato for pie filling to save some time.

Belton's Bacon Potatoes Au Gratin

You might have to put a seatbelt on your chair while you eat—these flavors will send you to the moon. Thanks to my mother, I never met a potato or a piece of bacon that I didn't like. So naturally, I put these together by instinct. Trust me, you will not be disappointed. *Serves 4 to 6*

½ pound bacon

2 tablespoons butter

3 cloves garlic, smashed

2 teaspoons Creole seasoning

1 teaspoon fresh thyme

1 tablespoon finely chopped fresh parsley

2 teaspoons kosher salt

1 teaspoon freshly cracked pepper

4 pounds Yukon gold or russet potatoes, peeled, rinsed, drained, sliced, and chilled for 10 minutes

2½ cups heavy cream

Preheat oven to 350 degrees.

In a sauté pan over medium heat, cook bacon until wilted and golden on each side, about 10 minutes, turning once. Remove and set aside to drain on a paper towel.

Heat butter in sauté pan. Add garlic and heat for 2 minutes to sweat the flavor. Remove from heat and coat the inside of a 9 x 9-inch baking dish with the garlic butter.

In a small bowl, combine the Creole seasoning, thyme, parsley, salt, and pepper.

Toss potatoes in seasoning to coat. Divide into thirds.

Place a layer of potatoes in the baking dish. Add a layer of bacon. Repeat, ending with a layer of potatoes. Pour cream over mixture and press down potatoes to release air and make sure cream penetrates all layers.

Place in oven and bake for 45 minutes. During the baking, at the 20 minute mark, reach into dish with wooden spoon and break the crust that is forming. After another 20 minutes, repeat. You will know that the dish is done when the top begins to brown. Remove from oven and cool for 20 minutes before serving.

TIPS & SUGGESTIONS

You can use prosciutto or ham if you prefer instead of the bacon.

POULTRY

Mom bought chickens at Schwegmann's. But, I also remember the butcher by my house on Freret Street having chickens. We'd just go over there and get them as needed. My cousin Lorna and I were reminiscing about shopping on Freret Street, and I got so tickled with her story. She told me that it took years for her to put two and two together.

Nan would take Lorna with her to the butcher, where she enjoyed seeing the chickens, ducks, turtles, and turkeys walking around in their pens. Lorna was always tasked with picking out the chicken. She explained that she loved to pick "her" chicken. Then they would leave the butcher's place to run errands—maybe they would stop in Long's Bakery to grab a snack or go over to the Canal Villere for a few sundries, and then they would pick up the chicken on the way back to the house. She said it took her years to make the connection that the live chicken she picked would be the butchered one they brought home and cooked for dinner. This just cracks me up.

Grandma Emily took her chicken very seriously. In her 7th Ward kitchen, she kept a separate preparation kit for her chicken tasks. I swear this is true. Knife, towel, scrub brush, scissors, and other sundries necessary to bring the chicken to a cleanliness level of her approval. She would put that chicken in the sink, and with her bottle scrubbing brush, she'd scrub the flavor out of that chicken. Under the wings. Inside. Outside. Only then could she work with it. Snipping. Clipping. Pulling stray feathers. Thinking back on it, I'm so impressed that she was tuned into the extra steps of care for ensuring that the chicken was prepared right. I also remember her soaking her tools in bleach and water afterwards. And, then packing up her tool kit ready for the next bird. Skill. And, care. That was my Grandma Emily.

CHICKEN CLEMENCEAU

*This is Chef Leah Chase's signature dish at Dooky Chase. I feel so lucky to have stood next to Chef Leah while she prepared this dish in her kitchen at the corner of Orleans and North Miro streets. I continue to be inspired by her as I believe she is truly the Grand Dame of Creole cooking. True story: I being a young, inexperienced chef asked Chef Leah if she ever put a little cream in this recipe. I'll never forget the look she gave me. I can interpret it clearly as a "no." And, I'll leave it at that. To this day, when I make classic Creole recipes, I remind myself of the lesson Chef Leah taught me that day. When something is great already, don't try to make it better. **Serves 4 to 6**

CHICKEN

1 whole chicken, cut into 8 pieces

1 tablespoon kosher salt

1 tablespoon pepper

BRABANT POTATOES

1/2 cup vegetable oil

2 large russet potatoes, peeled and diced

4 tablespoons clarified butter

1 pound button mushrooms, sliced

3 tablespoons minced garlic

3 tablespoons dry white wine

Salt, to taste

1 teaspoon white pepper

1/2 pound shelled English peas

Fresh parsley

CHICKEN

Preheat oven to 400 degrees.

Rinse chicken and pat dry. Season with salt and pepper and bake in a large glass baking dish for 30 minutes until chicken is golden brown. Turn after the first 15 minutes and season again.

BRABANT POTATOES

Heat oil in a large skillet to 350 degrees. Season potatoes with salt and pepper and fry in skillet until golden brown, about 8 minutes. Move cubes throughout the cooking process to ensure that they brown equally. Remove and drain on a paper towel.

In the same skillet on high heat, add butter and sauté mushrooms for about 5 minutes, until tender. Add garlic and sauté for 1 minute or until you smell the garlic aroma. Deglaze pan with wine. Reduce for 2 minutes. Add potatoes and sauté until heated through, about 5 minutes. Season with salt and white pepper. Add peas and continue to heat through. Adjust seasoning.

Remove from heat and divide the potatoes on the dinner plates. Top with chicken portions and garnish with parsley.

TIPS & SUGGESTIONS

Remember the advice Chef Leah Chase gave me: When something is great already, don't try to make it better.

LOUISIANA BOUDIN-STUFFED QUAIL

Boudin is a Cajun rice sausage that appears all over south Louisiana. Cut the casing and remove the rice, meat, and seasonings and you have a ready-made stuffing. **Serves 6 for an appetizer or 3 to 4 for dinner**

---

6 quail with breastbone removed

1½ pounds boudin sausage, casing removed

Kosher salt and freshly ground pepper, to taste

1 tablespoon Creole seasoning

12 strips maple-smoked bacon

Preheat oven to 350 degrees.

Stuff each quail with the boudin. Season the quail with salt, pepper, and Creole seasoning. Wrap with the bacon lengthwise to keep the boudin inside and secure the bacon with a toothpick.

Bake for 45 minutes, or until the bacon is crispy, in a large glass baking dish.

TIPS & SUGGESTIONS

If you use Cornish hens instead of quail, bake for an hour and 15 minutes. And, creamy garlic grits are a perfect accompaniment as the flavors from the juices of the cooked quail add another dimension to the grits.

SLOW ROASTED DUCK WITH ORANGE AND SOY SAUCE GRAVY

As a young man, my duck experiences were limited to duck in gumbo and a friend of mine's mother would fry it like chicken. It wasn't until my cousin Lorna decided to cook a whole duck for dinner one night that I became enlightened. Until then, I had never experienced the elegance of a roasted duck. I have to say that she really got it right. **Serves 4 to 6**

2 (2.5-pound) ducks, cleaned and patted dry

Salt and pepper, to taste

2 tablespoons butter

2 whole onions, halved and sliced

4 large rosemary sprigs

2 cups orange juice

1/4 cup soy sauce

1 cup tawny port

2 large carrots, peeled and cut on the bias

1/4 pound button mushrooms, sliced, or baby portobello mushrooms

8 ounces roasted red peppers, julienned

Parsley

Preheat oven to 475 degrees.

Place ducks in large roasting pan, side by side. Season with salt and pepper inside and out.

Melt butter in a large skillet on medium-high heat; add onions and quickly sauté for 2 minutes. Add rosemary sprigs and sauté for 1 minute; remove from heat. Using a slotted spoon, take out the onions and rosemary springs, leaving the melted butter, and place inside ducks.

Place ducks in hot oven for 12 minutes. Reduce heat to 275 degrees, cover loosely with aluminum foil, and roast for 4 hours. Check hourly to skim fat and set aside.

Remove from oven and remove as much of the fat as possible. Pour in orange juice, soy sauce, and port. Return ducks to oven and continue to cook for an additional 40 minutes. Remove ducks to a serving platter and let cool slightly.

Transfer pan juices to a sauce pan and bring to a boil over high heat. Add carrots and continue to cook until volume reduces to 1 1/2 cups. Once reduced, turn heat to medium and add mushrooms and red peppers and cook for 2 minutes. Remove from heat and season with salt and pepper. Serve over duck. Garnish with parsley.

TIPS & SUGGESTIONS

Serve with crispy Zapp's unsalted potato chips, our local New Orleans potato chip, or Brabant Potatoes (page 155) and orange slices.

Irish New Orleans

Dad's postman beat was Uptown New Orleans. He worked out of station B on Carondolet Street around Marengo and St. Charles. This happened to be right around the corner from the original Martin's Wine Cellar. Yes, we New Orleanians use food destinations as landmarks for direction.

I remember hearing him talk about the Irish Channel. He would be on the phone at the house and mention the Irish Channel. I was always like, "I gotta go see this Irish Channel." Hearing about people swimming the English Channel, I just created this vision of parallel significance. And, we are surrounded by water here. I mean, why not? For years and from the backseat of the car, I kept vigil for this body of water and never got to see it. I wonder why. Wink. Wink. That is my first memory of hearing about the Irish Channel as a child.

The actual boundaries of the Irish Channel in New Orleans are between Magazine Street, First Street, and Toledano Streets with the Mississippi River as the border. It was the neighborhood for Irish immigrants who came to New Orleans in the nineteenth century.

What was cool about the Irish Channel is that although predominantly Irish, it was mixed with Germans, Italians, and African Americans, right alongside the Irish. The architecture is amazing. And, to this day, it is still home to two amazing Irish bars, Tracey's and Parasol's, pretty much right next door to each other. And this area goes full Irish for the St. Patrick's Day parade. You can catch your cabbage, carrots, and potatoes for your Irish stew at the Irish Day Parade, compliments of the thousands of riders on the endless floats—a celebration that rivals a Mardi Gras parade.

Irish food didn't escape our Creole household. I remember Mom making what she called Irish stew during the cooler months as a hearty and flavorful one-dish dinner filled with meat and potatoes. And, Grandma Emily made the best Shepherd's Pie with ground lamb and Cottage Pie with beef. Her potato topping was a knockout. In October, once the weather cooled off, these wonderful hearty dishes would appear on the kitchen table and hang around until March for St. Patty's Day.

CREOLE COTTAGE PIE

When you break through the seal of the mashed potato topping and reach the simmering goodness of beef and vegetables, you realize what is special about this slow cooked dish.

Serves 6 to 8

CASSEROLE

I tablespoon vegetable oil

1 large onion, finely diced

1 teaspoon pepper

4 large carrots, finely chopped

1 cup chopped button mushrooms

1 cup fresh English peas

1 pound ground beef

5 ounces dry red wine

2 tablespoons tomato paste

3 tablespoons Worcestershire sauce

1 cup vegetable stock

1 teaspoon salt

2 teaspoons fresh thyme

2 tablespoons butter

2 tablespoons all-purpose flour

¼ cup chopped parsley

TOPPING

5 cups Classic Mashed Potatoes

1 egg, beaten

1 cup grated white cheddar cheese, divided

CASSEROLE

Preheat oven to 350 degrees.

In a large sauté pan, heat oil over medium-high heat. Add onion and pepper. Sauté for 5 minutes until translucent. Add carrots and continue to sauté for 3 minutes. Add mushrooms and peas and stir. Continue to sauté for 2 minutes. Remove vegetables.

Add ground beef and brown thoroughly. Add wine and tomato paste. Continue to cook until wine is reduced, about 5 minutes. Add Worcestershire, stock, salt, and thyme. Continue to simmer until reduced by half, about 2 minutes. Return vegetables to pan and stir. Add butter and flour and stir to thicken, about 1 minute. Add parsley and then remove from heat.

Coat a large glass or ceramic baking dish with nonstick cooking spray. Spoon in meat filling and evenly spread in dish.

TOPPING

Combine potatoes, egg, and ½ cup of the cheese. Spread evenly over meat. Top with remaining cheese.

Bake for 20 minutes or until meat filling is simmering. You can place in broiler to brown the top, if desired.

TIPS & SUGGESTIONS

Pipe the mashed potatoes over the top using a pastry bag and large tip. This adds a little character to the pie. To make shepherd's pie, use ground lamb instead of beef.

CLASSIC MASHED POTATOES

Makes 5 to 6 cups

4 pounds russet potatoes, evenly chopped and rinsed

1 teaspoon salt

$^1/_2$ cup butter

2 cups whole milk or 1 cup whole milk and 1 cup heavy cream mixed

Salt and pepper, to taste

In a large stockpot, add potatoes and cover entirely with water. Add salt and stir. Bring to a boil and boil for 20 minutes or until potatoes are fork tender. Drain through a colander and return potatoes to hot pan. Add butter and stir to incorporate until butter is melted. Slowly add milk and mash until the desired thickness is achieved. For a completely smooth mash, you can use an electric mixer. Adjust seasoning and serve.

TIPS & SUGGESTIONS

If you use red potatoes, you can leave a little skin for texture and character. Your potatoes need to be very smooth so you can easily layer on the top of the pie.

New Orleans Irish Stew

You can go to any of the great Uptown or Downtown Irish parades and get all of the ingredients except the meat for this stew. **Serves 4 to 6**

---

3 tablespoons vegetable oil

2 pounds stew meat, cut into 1-inch pieces

2 large onions, cut into ¼-inch slices

5 cloves garlic, minced

2 tablespoons dried thyme

3 tablespoons tomato paste

1 pint ale

4 cups beef stock

1 tablespoon sugar

3 bay leaves

3 tablespoons butter

3 carrots, sliced in rounds

4 large potatoes, cubed

2 cups sliced cabbage

2 tablespoons chopped Italian parsley

In a large stockpot over medium heat, heat oil. Add beef and brown on all sides. You might need to do this in 2 batches. It will take about 5 minutes for each batch to brown. Remove and set aside.

Add onions and sauté about 3 minutes until translucent. Add garlic and thyme and continue to sauté until garlic releases oils, about 1 minute. Add tomato paste and continue to sauté for 1 minute. Add beef back into mixture and continue to sauté until browned, about 4 minutes.

Deglaze with ale. Add stock, sugar, and bay leaves. Bring to a boil and reduce to a simmer.

In a sauté pan, heat butter and sauté carrots and potatoes until golden brown, about 15 minutes. Add cabbage and sauté until slightly wilted, about 3 minutes.

Add sautéed vegetables to stock pot and cook through before serving. Garnish with parsley.

TIPS & SUGGESTIONS

Serve with Irish Channel Soda Bread (facing page).

IrISH CHannel soDa BreaD

I am so accustomed to the light, airy texture of French bread. But as a realist, I understand my beloved, delicate French bread is no match for these hearty Irish dishes. Crafted by Irish housewives without access to yeast, these industrious cooks created a quick bread that holds up to the hearty stews and cottage pie dishes. Irish soda bread is a great complement to these dishes and super easy to make. **Makes 1 large loaf**

---

3 ½ cups all-purpose flour

4 tablespoons sugar

1 teaspoon baking soda

1 teaspoon kosher salt

1 ¾ cups cold buttermilk

1 cup raisins, optional (not traditional)

Preheat oven to 425 degrees. Prepare a baking sheet by lightly flouring.

Mix flour, sugar, baking soda, and salt thoroughly together. Slowly add buttermilk and mix to form wet clumps. Add raisins, if using.

On a lightly floured work surface, gather dough into a ball and knead until dough holds, about 1 minute. Be careful not to overwork or bread will be hard.

Place on baking sheet, score top with an "X." Bake until browned and when tapped sounds hollow. Remove from oven and cool completely.

TIPS anD suggesTIons

One tablespoon of lemon juice or white vinegar in a cup of milk is a solid substitute for buttermilk in this recipe. Be sure to let it stand for 5 minutes before using.

Reveillon Dinner

Reveillion is the French word for awakening and refers to a tradition that celebrates with an often elaborate dinner or party the night before Christmas Day and New Year's Eve. Reveillion was traditionally celebrated by the Catholics of New Orleans of French decent. They would return home from midnight mass and enjoy this elaborate dinner at home. Reveillion went passé for a time. But the tradition of enjoying a great meal the night before Christmas has morphed into something else here in New Orleans. Having come up as an alter boy, and with my dad being Catholic, we stayed up for midnight mass and we'd have a big dinner that same night. That's how you came up in New Orleans.

The idea of Reveillon emerged again in the 1980s and has grown where restaurants around the city embrace the idea and offer terrific traditional multi-course menus that evoke the spirit of the season for the month of December. It's a great way to preserve this culinary tradition.

For me, I love the holidays and the time spent at home with family and friends. Christmas wasn't complete without a visit to Auntie Lois and Uncle Mitch's house. We always ended up there in the evenings to finish off the day with desserts and opening presents. After knocking off cakes, pies, and ice cream, my cousins Demetria, Hank, Byron, William, Monique, Trevor, and I would be sent outside until the sugar rush wore off.

One of my memorable Reveillon dinners was prepared by my dear friend Norma and her husband, Captain Gary Bair. I met them in 1991 at The New Orleans School of Cooking shortly after they were stationed at the Algiers Naval Support Base on the Westbank, across the river from the French Quarter. Norma, already an accomplished cook, dove right into New Orleans food, and to this day, I believe she elevated cooking to an art and really touched everyone who was privileged to dine at her table. Norma's Reveillion dinners were, in my opinion, the Super Bowl of food events. And, that's saying a lot from an ex-football player.

SMOTHERED CREOLE PORK ROAST

Pork roast really needs to cook low and slow. Treat it tender and delicately. This isn't a dish that needs to be rushed. My mom would cook this type of dish on Saturdays and Sundays when she had the time to leave it in the oven. *Serves 12*

---

1 (6-pound) boneless pork roast (butt or shoulder is fine)

1 tablespoon kosher salt

1 tablespoon freshly cracked pepper

2 cups thinly sliced yellow onion

10 cloves garlic, chopped

2 tablespoons fresh thyme

1 tablespoon chopped fresh rosemary

1 tablespoon Creole seasoning

3 tablespoons vegetable oil

1/2 cup unsalted butter

1/2 cup all-purpose flour

4 cups chicken stock

Cooked rice

1/4 cup chopped parsley

Preheat oven to 275 degrees.

Season the roast generously with salt and pepper. In a large bowl, mix onions, garlic, thyme, rosemary, and Creole seasoning.

In a large Dutch oven, heat oil on high heat. Sear the roast and brown on all sides, about 15 minutes turning to keep the roast from burning. Remove from pan and set aside.

Reduce heat to medium and stir in butter. When butter is melted, add flour to form a roux. Stir constantly until the roux darkens to the color of peanut butter, about 10 minutes.

Add onion mixture to roux and cook until coated and wilted, about 4 minutes. Slowly add stock and whisk to remove lumps. Simmer for 5 minutes. Add roast and spoon the broth over the top of the roast to saturate and cover with onions. Cover and cook for 3 hours, basting every 30 minutes as well as turning roast, until the meat is tender and breaks apart easily.

Remove from oven and serve over rice and garnish with parsley.

TIP & SUGGESTIONS

Seasoning the roast the night before gives more time for the flavors to infuse.

REDFISH SAUCE PIQUANTE

Uncle Chet would bring my mother big ol' redfish. My mom said the big fish, because of their age, could sometimes be too tough to filet. She'd just have him scale and gut it and bring it whole. Then, she would cook a huge amount of this sauce. She always layered the bottom of a big turkey roaster with the sauce and would place the whole redfish simply seasoned with salt and pepper right on top. To finish, she would then top the fish with more sauce. The fish was super tender after about an hour and a half. When she lifted the lid and you saw the fish swimming in that sauce, you thought, "Oh my, this is gonna be so good." I created this recipe using filets because finding the whole redfish can be challenging when you live away from the coast. **Serves 4 to 6**

¼ cup vegetable oil

6 (8-ounce) redfish or drum filets

½ cup diced yellow onion

¼ cup diced celery

¼ cup diced green bell pepper

4 cloves fresh garlic, minced

¼ cup minced Italian parsley

1 teaspoon red pepper

2 tablespoons Creole seasoning

½ teaspoon cayenne pepper

6 ounces tomato paste

32 ounces chicken broth

¼ cup dry red wine

3 bay leaves

2 cups chopped fresh tomatoes

8 ounces tomato sauce

1 tablespoon hot sauce

Zest of 1 lemon and lemon slices

Cooked rice

1 cup chopped green onions

Heat oil in a large Dutch oven over medium heat. Brown filets on both sides, remove, and set aside.

Add onion, celery, bell pepper, garlic, and parsley. Sauté until cooked, about 10 minutes. Add red pepper, Creole seasoning, and cayenne and sauté for 1 minute. Add tomato paste and continue to cook until browned, about 3–4 minutes.

Deglaze pan with broth and wine. Add bay leaves, tomatoes, tomato sauce, hot sauce, and zest and cook until the sauce begins to thicken, about 5 minutes.

Reduce heat to low, cover, and cook for 20 minutes to reduce sauce and marry flavors. Check often to prevent scorching.

After 30 minutes, remove cover and gently add filets to sauce. Simply lay them on top. Cover again and keep flame on low. Cook for 10–12 minutes until fish is cooked through (it will steam in covered pan with juices from sauce).

Serve over rice and garnish with lemon and green onion.

TIPS & SUGGESTIONS

My recipe calls for filets. The recipe remains the same whether you are using whole fish or filets. There are a few simple changes for the whole fish in this recipe. First of all you don't have to brown the whole fish. Simply place on the sauce. Top with more sauce and cook for about 1 hour covered, just like my mom did. You can also use trout as a fish substitute.

BÛCHE DE NOËL

Considered to be the grand finale of a Revellion dinner, it's also called a yule log. This cake looks more complicated than it really is. So my words of advice, "I'm a chef, not a baker. If I can pull this off, you can, too." This is really the spirit of New Orleans cooking. Just give it a try.
Serves 12 to 14

BASIC YELLOW CAKE

3 eggs

1 cup sugar

1/3 cup water

1 teaspoon vanilla

3/4 cup all-purpose flour

1 teaspoon baking powder

1/4 teaspoon salt

CREAM FILLING

1 cup heavy cream

2 tablespoons sugar

1 cup fresh raspberry preserves

CHOCOLATE FROSTING

1/3 cup unsweetened cocoa powder

6 tablespoons butter, softened

2 cups powdered sugar

1 1/2 teaspoons vanilla

2 tablespoons hot water

GARNISH

Powdered sugar

Chopped nuts and holiday flourish

BASIC YELLOW CAKE

Preheat oven to 375 degrees. Line a 10 x 15-inch cake pan with parchment paper. Grease with nonstick cooking spray.

Beat eggs in a large bowl on high speed using an electric mixer for 5 minutes or until thick and bright yellow. Gradually add sugar and continue to mix. Add water and vanilla and continue to mix on low speed. Add flour, baking powder, and salt and gently beat until the batter is smooth, about 5 minutes. Pour into pan and spread evenly.

Bake for 15 minutes or until it passes the toothpick test. (Toothpick inserted in center comes out clean.)

Remove from oven to cool by sliding parchment, with cake still on top, off of the pan and onto the countertop. You only want to cool for 10-15 minutes because you need the cake to remain flexible. If it is too cool, you won't be able to roll it. It will crack and fall apart.

CREAM FILLING

While cake is cooling, beat whipping cream and sugar. Set aside and hold preserves.

CHOCOLATE FROSTING

While cake continues to cool, start the frosting. In a medium bowl, beat cocoa and butter on low speed. Add powdered sugar and thoroughly mix. Add vanilla and continue to mix. Slowly add water until frosting is smooth, glossy, and easy to spread.

Take your hand and run it under the warm cake to loosen it from the parchment.

Spread the preserves, leaving an inch of cake on each end uncoated. Follow with a thin layer of cream, careful to leave about an inch uncoated at the end. Turn the cake so it is in position to easily roll up. Use the parchment paper to help you lift the cake and begin the roll. Once you've rolled the cake, in one swift move, pick up the roll and transfer to a serving plate, making sure the end of the roll is on the bottom to keep the cake rolled up and in place.

Frost the roll and score with a fork to look like bark. Sprinkle with powdered sugar and nuts and serve.

TIPS & SUGGESTIONS

You can chill this cake if you like. Make sure you dip the cutting knife in hot water before slicing to make a clean cut. I scored the chocolate icing so the cake looked like a real log. Use your inspiration. It is delicious with chicory coffee.

Resources

To view episodes of *New Orleans Cooking with Kevin Belton visit:*

WYES TV
916 Navarre Avenue
New Orleans, LA 70124
504-486-5511
www.wyes.org

For Chef Kevin's Creole Seasoning and other hard-to-find spices and Louisiana products:

The New Orleans School of Cooking and Louisiana General Store
524 St. Louis Street
New Orleans, LA 70130
504-525-2665
800-237-4841
www.neworleansschoolofcooking.com

For Louisiana meats and sausages like boudin, andouille, and smoked Creole sausages as well as other items:

The Best Stop Supermarket, Inc.
615 Highway 93 N.
Scott, LA 70583
337-233-5805
www.beststopinscott.com

For Louisiana seafood, especially shrimp, crawfish tails, crabs, and other specialty items:

Louisiana Seafood Exchange
428 Jefferson Highway
Jefferson, LA 70121
504-834-9393
800-969-9394
www.louisianaseafoodexchange.net

Authentic King Cakes

Manny Randazzo King Cakes
3515 N. Hullen Street
Metairie, LA 70002
504-456-1476
866-456-1476
www.randazzokingcake.com

INDEX

12th Night King Cake, 112

A
Amandine, Soft Shell Crab, 90
apple, in Red Cabbage, 62
artichoke:
    Artichoke Bottoms, 70, 71
    Eggs Sardou, 70
    Oyster and Artichoke Soup, 98
avocado, in Traditionally Classic
    Guacamole, 39

B
bacon:
    Beef Rouladen, 59
    Belton's Bacon Potatoes Au Gratin, 153
    Creole Daube, 122
    Creole Potato Salad, 111
    Fried Oysters and Spinach Salad with
        Fresh Ponchatoula Strawberries, 130
    Louisiana Cornbread, 101
    Praline Bacon Sprinkles, 49
    Red Cabbage, 62
    Smothered Greens with Pecan-Smoked
        Bacon, 102
Banana Pudding, 106
Bananas Foster, New Orleans, 25
Barbecue Spareribs, Kevin's Dry and
    Wet, 104
Barbecue Shrimp, New Orleans-Style, 68
Basic Shrimp Stock, 108
Beans and Rice, Red, 140
Beans, Miss Magnolia Battle's Southern-
    Style Butter, 52
beef:
    Beef Rouladen, 59
    Creole Cottage Pie, 160
    Creole Daube, 122
    Kevin's NOLA New Year's Corned Beef, 55
    Larded Roast, 123
    Louisiana Boudin-Stuffed Quail, 156
    New Orleans Irish Stew, 162
    Stuffed Green Bell Peppers, 44
    Triple Threat Meatballs, 84
Beef Rouladen, 59
beer:
    New Orleans Irish Stew, 162
    New Orleans-Style Barbecue Shrimp, 68
    Thin-Fried Beer-Battered Catfish, 118
Beignets, French Quarter, 19

bell pepper:
    green:
        Chef Kevin's Jambalaya à la Big
            Easy, 32
        Clean-Out-the-Fridge Frittata, 74
        Corn and Sweet Pepper Relish, 145
        Corn Maque Choux, 23
        Crab Cakes, 89
        Crabmeat-Stuffed Shrimp, 92
        Crawfish and Corn Bisque, 94
        Creole Okra, 146
        Dirty Rice, 136
        Grillades and Grits, 26
        Happy New Year's Cabbage
            Casserole, 54
        Lorna's Oyster Patties, 127
        New Orleans Shrimp Étouffée, 78
        Redfish Sauce Piquante, 166
        Seafood Gumbo, 20
        Shrimp and Andouille Gumbo, 108
        Shrimp Creole, 65
        Stuffed Green Bell Peppers, 44
        Stuffed Mirliton, 134
        Turtle Soup, 96
    red, in Corn and Sweet Pepper Relish, 145
    yellow, Clean-Out-the-Fridge Frittata, 74
Belton's Bacon Potatoes Au Gratin, 153
Bisque, Crab and Corn, 77
Bisque, Crawfish and Corn, 94
Black-Eyed Peas and Andouille, 57
Blender Hollandaise Sauce, 73
blueberries, in Nan's Saturday Buttermilk
    Pancakes with Praline Bacon
    Sprinkles, 48
bread:
    French bread:
        Bread Pudding with Whiskey
            Sauce, 143
        Chef Kevin's New Orleans-Glazed
            Ham Po'Boys, 50
        New Orleans-Style Barbecue
            Shrimp, 68
        New Orleans-Style Eggs Benedict, 72
        Pain Perdu, 28
    Irish Channel Soda Bread, 163
Bread Pudding with Whiskey Sauce, 143
breadcrumbs:
    Crab Cakes, 89
    Crabmeat-Stuffed Shrimp, 92

Fried Green Tomatoes, 148
Oysters Rockefeller, 128
Paneed Veal, 139
Pecan-Crusted Redfish, 115
Stuffed Mirliton, 134
Triple Threat Meatballs, 84
broccoli, in Clean-Out-the-Fridge Frittata, 74
Bûche de Noël, 168
Butter Beans, Miss Magnolia Battle's
    Southern-Style, 52
buttermilk: see milk
butternut squash, in Clean-Out-the-Fridge
    Frittata, 74

C
cabbage:
    Happy New Year's Cabbage Casserole, 54
    New Orleans Irish Stew, 162
    Red Cabbage, 62
Cake, 12th Night King, 112
Calas, Traditional New Orleans, 31
carrot:
    Basic Shrimp Stock, 108
    Creole Cottage Pie, 160
    Creole Daube, 122
    Kevin's NOLA New Year's Corned Beef, 55
    New Orleans Irish Stew, 162
    Slow Roasted Duck with Orange and
        Soy Sauce Gravy, 158
casserole:
    Creole Cottage Pie, 160
    Happy New Year's Cabbage Casserole, 54
    Sweet Potato Pecan Casserole, 151
celery:
    Basic Shrimp Stock, 108
    Chef Kevin's Jambalaya à la Big Easy, 32
    Classic Rich Red Rémoulade, 67
    Corn and Sweet Pepper Relish, 145
    Crab Cakes, 89
    Crabmeat-Stuffed Shrimp, 92
    Crawfish and Corn Bisque, 94
    Creole Potato Salad, 111
    Dirty Rice, 136
    Happy New Year's Cabbage Casserole, 54
    Kevin's NOLA New Year's Corned Beef, 55
    Lorna's Oyster Patties, 127
    New Orleans Shrimp Étouffée, 78
    Oyster and Artichoke Soup, 98
    Red Beans and Rice, 140
    Redfish Sauce Piquante, 166

Seafood Gumbo, 20
Shrimp and Andouille Gumbo, 108
Shrimp Creole, 65
Stuffed Green Bell Peppers, 44
Stuffed Mirliton, 134
Turtle Soup, 96
White Rémoulade, 66
cheese:
    cheddar:
        Chef Kevin's New Orleans-Glazed
            Ham Po'Boys, 50
        Creole Cottage Pie, 160
        Stuffed Green Bell Peppers, 44
    cream cheese, in 12th Night King Cake, 112
    Feta, Sweet Potato Gnocchi with Sage
        and, 150
    mascarpone:
        Mascarpone Cream, 86
        Tiramisu Cupcakes, 86
    Parmesan:
        Oysters Rockefeller, 128
        Spaghetti Bordelaise, 125
        Sweet Potato Gnocchi with Sage and
            Feta, 150
        Triple Threat Meatballs, 84
    ricotta, in Sweet Potato Gnocchi with
        Sage and Feta, 150
Chef Kevin's Down-Home Dry Rub, 104
Chef Kevin's Jambalaya à la Big Easy, 32
Chef Kevin's New Orleans-Glazed Ham
    Po'Boys, 50
Chef Kevin's Sunday Morning Cure
    (Pazole), 38
Chef Kevin's Wet Barbecue Sauce, 105
chicken: see poultry
Chicken Clemenceau, 155
Chile Sauce, 38
Classic Mashed Potatoes, 161
Classic Rich Red Rémoulade, 67
Clean-Out-the-Fridge Frittata, 74
Coastal Taco-lade Sauce, 36
corn:
    Corn and Sweet Pepper Relish, 145
    Corn Maque Choux, 23
    Crab and Corn Bisque, 77
    Crawfish and Corn Bisque, 94
    Fresh Creamed Corn, 95
    Louisiana Cornbread, 101
Corn and Sweet Pepper Relish, 145
Corn Maque Choux, 23
cornbread:
    Happy New Year's Cabbage Casserole, 54
    Louisiana Cornbread, 101
Corned Beef, Kevin's NOLA New Year's, 55
Crab and Corn Bisque, 77

Crab Cakes, 89
crab claw: see seafood
crabmeat: see seafood
Crabmeat-Stuffed Shrimp, 92
Crawfish and Corn Bisque, 94
Creamed Spinach, 71
Creole Cottage Pie, 160
Creole Daube, 122
Creole Okra, 146
Creole Potato Salad, 111
Creole Tartar Sauce, 119
Crisps, Homemade Tortilla, 40
Cupcakes, Tiramisu, 86

D
Dirty Rice, 136
Dry-Brined Turkey, 133
duck: see poultry

E
Eggs Benedict, New Orleans-Style, 72
Eggs Sardou, 70
evaporated milk: see milk

F
Fish Tacos with Coastal Taco-lade Sauce, 36
French Quarter Beignets, 19
Fresh Creamed Corn, 95
Fried Green Tomatoes, 148
Fried Oysters and Spinach Salad with Fresh
    Ponchatoula Strawberries, 130
Frittata, Clean-Out-the-Fridge, 74

G
green onion:
    Black-Eyed Peas and Andouille, 57
    Classic Rich Red Rémoulade, 67
    Coastal Taco-lade Sauce, 36
    Corn Maque Choux, 23
    Crab and Corn Bisque, 77
    Crab Cakes, 89
    Crabmeat-Stuffed Shrimp, 92
    Crawfish and Corn Bisque, 94
    Creole Potato Salad, 111
    Dirty Rice, 136
    Gumbo Seafood, 20
    New Orleans Shrimp Étouffée, 78
    New Orleans-Style Barbecue Shrimp, 68
    Oyster and Artichoke Soup, 98
    Oysters Rockefeller, 128
    Red Beans and Rice, 140
    Redfish Sauce Piquante, 166
    Shrimp Creole, 65
    Spaghetti Bordelaise, 125
    Turtle Soup, 96
    White Rémoulade, 66

Greens with Pecan-Smoked Bacon,
    Smothered, 102
Grillades and Grits, 26
Guacamole, Traditionally Classic, 39
Gumbo, Seafood, 20
Gumbo, Shrimp and Andouille, 108

H
ham: see pork
Happy New Year's Cabbage Casserole, 54
heavy cream: see milk
Herbsaint Dressing, 130
Homemade Tortilla Crisps, 40
hominy, in Chef Kevin's Sunday Morning
    Cure (Pazole), 38

I
Irish Channel Soda Bread, 163

J
Jambalaya à la Big Easy, Chef Kevin's, 32

K
Kevin's Creole Rice Custard Pudding, 34
Kevin's Dry and Wet Barbecue Spareribs, 104
Kevin's NOLA New Year's Corned Beef, 55

L
Larded Roast, 123
lemon:
    12th Night King Cake, 112
    Artichoke Bottoms, 71
    Blender Hollandaise Sauce, 73
    Chef Kevin's New Orleans-Glazed Ham
        Po'Boys, 50
    Crabmeat-Stuffed Shrimp, 92
    Creole Tartar Sauce, 119
    Lemon Crème Brûlée, 121
    Lorna's Oyster Patties, 127
    Oysters Rockefeller, 128
    Pecan-Crusted Redfish, 115
    Redfish Sauce Piquante, 166
    Shrimp Rémoulade, 66
    Soft Shell Crab Amandine, 90
    Thin-Fried Beer-Battered Catfish, 118
    Trout Meunière, 117
    Turtle Soup, 96
    White Rémoulade, 66
Lemon Crème Brûlée, 121
lettuce:
    Chef Kevin's New Orleans-Glazed Ham
        Po'Boys, 50
    Shrimp Rémoulade, 66
liqueur:
    anise liqueur, in Oysters Rockefeller, 128

banana liqueur, in New Orleans
    Bananas Foster, 25
coffee liqueur, in Tiramisu Cupcakes, 86
Herbsaint liqueur, in Herbsaint
    Dressing, 130
Lorna's Oyster Patties, 127
Louisiana Boudin-Stuffed Quail, 156
Louisiana Cornbread, 101
Louisiana Pecan Pie, 137

M

mayonnaise:
    Crab Cakes, 89
    Crabmeat-Stuffed Shrimp, 92
    Creole Potato Salad, 111
    Creole Tartar Sauce, 119
    Herbsaint Dressing, 130
    White Rémoulade, 66
Meatballs, Triple Threat, 84
milk:
    buttermilk:
        Fried Green Tomatoes, 148
        Herbsaint Dressing, 130
        Irish Channel Soda Bread, 163
        Nan's Saturday Buttermilk Pancakes
            with Praline Bacon Sprinkles, 48
    condensed milk, in Banana Pudding, 106
    evaporated milk:
        French Quarter Beignets, 19
        Sweet Potato Pie, 46
    half-and-half:
        Crab and Corn Bisque, 77
        Crawfish and Corn Bisque, 94
        Fresh Creamed Corn, 95
        Louisiana Cornbread, 101
        New Orleans-Style Fried Chicken, 43
        Oyster and Artichoke Soup, 98
    heavy cream:
        Banana Pudding, 106
        Belton's Bacon Potatoes Au Gratin, 153
        Bûche de Noël, 168
        Corn Maque Choux, 23
        Herbsaint Dressing, 130
        Lemon Crème Brûlée, 121
        Lorna's Oyster Patties, 127
        Tiramisu Cupcakes, 86
        Traditional Creole Louisiana Pecan
            Praline, 80
    milk:
        12th Night King Cake, 112
        Bread Pudding with Whiskey
            Sauce, 143
        Fried Oysters and Spinach Salad
            with Fresh Ponchatoula
            Strawberries, 130

whole milk:
    Banana Pudding, 106
    Classic Mashed Potatoes, 161
    Crab and Corn Bisque, 77
    Creamed Spinach, 71
    Fresh Creamed Corn, 95
    Kevin's Creole Rice Custard
        Pudding, 34
    Pain Perdu, 28
    Paneed Veal, 139
    Pecan-Crusted Redfish, 115
    Sweet Potato Pecan Casserole, 151
    Tiramisu Cupcakes, 86
    Triple Threat Meatballs, 84
Miss Magnolia Battle's Southern-Style
    Butter Beans, 52
mushroom:
    Brabant Potatoes, 155
    Chicken Clemenceau, 155
    Clean-Out-the-Fridge Frittata, 74
    Creole Cottage Pie, 160
    Lorna's Oyster Patties, 127
    Slow Roasted Duck with Orange and
        Soy Sauce Gravy, 158

N

Nan's Saturday Buttermilk Pancakes with
    Praline Bacon Sprinkles, 48
New Orleans Shrimp Étouffée, 78
New Orleans Bananas Foster, 25
New Orleans Irish Stew, 162
New Orleans-Style Barbecue Shrimp, 68
New Orleans-Style Eggs Benedict, 72
New Orleans-Style Fried Chicken, 43
Nilla Wafers, in Banana Pudding, 106
nut:
    almond, in Soft Shell Crab Amandine, 90
    pecan:
        Bread Pudding with Whiskey
            Sauce, 143
        Louisiana Pecan Pie, 137
        Pecan-Crusted Redfish, 115
        Praline Bacon Sprinkles, 49
        Roasted Louisiana Pecans, 80
        Sweet Potato Pecan Casserole, 151
        Traditional Creole Louisiana Pecan
            Praline, 80

O

okra:
    Creole Okra, 146
    Seafood Gumbo, 20
onion:
    Basic Shrimp Stock, 108
    Beef Rouladen, 59

Black-Eyed Peas and Andouille, 57
Chef Kevin's Jambalaya à la Big Easy, 32
Chef Kevin's Sunday Morning Cure
    (Pazole), 38
Clean-Out-the-Fridge Frittata, 74
Corn and Sweet Pepper Relish, 145
Corn Maque Choux, 23
Crab and Corn Bisque, 77
Crawfish and Corn Bisque, 94
Creamed Spinach, 71
Creole Cottage Pie, 160
Creole Okra, 146
Dirty Rice, 136
Fried Oysters and Spinach Salad with
    Fresh Ponchatoula Strawberries, 130
Happy New Year's Cabbage Casserole, 54
Kevin's NOLA New Year's Corned Beef, 55
Lorna's Oyster Patties, 127
Miss Magnolia Battle's Southern-Style
    Butter Beans, 52
New Orleans Irish Stew, 162
New Orleans Shrimp Étouffée, 78
Potato Pancakes, 60
Red Beans and Rice, 140
Red Cabbage, 62
Red Gravy New Orleans Style, 83
Redfish Sauce Piquante, 166
Seafood Gumbo, 20
Shrimp and Andouille Gumbo, 108
Shrimp Creole, 65
Shrimp Rémoulade, 66
Slow Roasted Duck with Orange and
    Soy Sauce Gravy, 158
Smothered Creole Pork Roast, 165
Smothered Greens with Pecan-Smoked
    Bacon, 102
Stuffed Green Bell Peppers, 44
Stuffed Mirliton, 134
Thin-Fried Beer-Battered Catfish, 118
Traditionally Classic Guacamole, 39
Triple Threat Meatballs, 84
Turtle Soup, 96
Oyster and Artichoke Soup, 98
Oysters Rockefeller, 128

P

Pain Perdu, 28
pancake:
    Nan's Saturday Buttermilk Pancakes
        with Praline Bacon Sprinkles, 48
    Potato Pancakes, 60
Paneed Veal, 139
(Pazole), Chef Kevin's Sunday Morning
    Cure, 38

pea:
    Brabant Potatoes, 155
    Chicken Clemenceau, 155
    Creole Cottage Pie, 160
Pecan Praline, Traditional Creole Louisiana, 80
Pecan-Crusted Redfish, 115
pickled jalepeño pepper, in Louisiana Cornbread, 101
pickled meat:
    Black-Eyed Peas and Andouille, 57
    Creole Daube, 122
    Larded Roast, 123
    Miss Magnolia Battle's Southern-Style Butter Beans, 52
    Red Beans and Rice, 140
pie:
    Louisiana Pecan Pie, 137
    Sweet Potato Pie, 46
Po'Boys, Chef Kevin's New Orleans-Glazed Ham, 50
Pork Roast, Smothered Creole, 165
potato:
    Belton's Bacon Potatoes Au Gratin, 153
    Brabant Potatoes, 155
    Chicken Clemenceau, 155
    Classic Mashed Potatoes, 161
    Creole Cottage Pie, 160
    Creole Potato Salad, 111
    New Orleans Irish Stew, 162
    Potato Pancakes, 60
Potato Pancakes, 60
pork:
    cutlet, in Grillades and Grits, 26
    ground, in Triple Threat Meatballs, 84
    ham:
        Chef Kevin's New Orleans-Glazed Ham Po'Boys, 50
        Eggs Sardou, 70
        New Orleans-Style Eggs Benedict, 72
    ribs, in Kevin's Dry and Wet Barbecue Spareribs, 104
    roast:
        Chef Kevin's Sunday Morning Cure (Pazole), 38
        Smothered Creole Pork Roast, 165
    sausage, in Dirty Rice, 136
port, tawny, in Slow Roasted Duck with Orange and Soy Sauce Gravy, 158
poultry:
    chicken:
        Chef Kevin's Jambalaya à la Big Easy, 32
        Chicken Clemenceau, 155
    Dirty Rice, 136
    New Orleans-Style Fried Chicken, 43
    Duck with Orange and Soy Sauce Gravy, Slow Roasted, 158
    Quail, Louisiana Boudin-Stuffed, 156
    Turkey, Dry-Brined, 133
Praline Bacon Sprinkles, 49
Pudding, Kevin's Creole Rice Custard, 34

Q

quail: see poultry

R

raisin:
    Bread Pudding with Whiskey Sauce, 143
    Kevin's Creole Rice Custard Pudding, 34
Red Beans and Rice, 140
Red Cabbage, 62
Red Gravy New Orleans Style, 83
red pepper, in Slow Roasted Duck with Orange and Soy Sauce Gravy, 158
redfish: see seafood
Redfish Sauce Piquante, 166
Relish, Corn and Sweet Pepper, 145
rémoulade:
    Classic Rich Red Rémoulade, 67
    Shrimp Rémoulade, 66
    White Rémoulade, 66
rice:
    Black-Eyed Peas and Andouille, 57
    Chef Kevin's Jambalaya à la Big Easy, 32
    Dirty Rice, 136
    Kevin's Creole Rice Custard Pudding, 34
    New Orleans Shrimp Étouffée, 78
    Red Beans and Rice, 140
    Redfish Sauce Piquante, 166
    Seafood Gumbo, 20
    Shrimp Creole, 65
    Smothered Creole Pork Roast, 165
    Stuffed Green Bell Peppers, 44
    Traditional New Orleans Calas, 31
Rice Custard Pudding, Kevin's Creole, 34
Roasted Louisiana Pecans, 80
root beer, in Chef Kevin's New Orleans-Glazed Ham Po'Boys, 50
Rouladen, Beef, 59
roux, 14
rum, in New Orleans Bananas Foster, 25

S

Salad with Fresh Ponchatoula Strawberries, Fried Oysters and Spinach, 130
sauce:
    Chef Kevin's Wet Barbecue Sauce, 105
    Chile Sauce, 38
    Classic Rich Red Rémoulade, 67
    Coastal Taco-lade Sauce, 36
    Whiskey Sauce, 143
    White Rémoulade, 66
sausage:
    Black-Eyed Peas and Andouille, 57
    Chef Kevin's Jambalaya à la Big Easy, 32
    Happy New Year's Cabbage Casserole, 54
    Louisiana Boudin-Stuffed Quail, 156
    Seafood Gumbo, 20
    Shrimp and Andouille Gumbo, 108
scallion, in Chef Kevin's Jambalaya à la Big Easy, 32
seafood:
    Catfish, Thin-Fried Beer-Battered, 118
    Crab Amandine, Soft Shell, 90
    crab claw, in Seafood Gumbo, 20
    crabmeat:
        Crab and Corn Bisque, 77
        Crab Cakes, 89
        Crabmeat-Stuffed Shrimp, 92
        Seafood Gumbo, 20
        Stuffed Mirliton, 134
    Crawfish and Corn Bisque, 94
    oyster:
        Fried Oysters and Spinach Salad with Fresh Ponchatoula Strawberries, 130
        Lorna's Oyster Patties, 127
        Oyster and Artichoke Soup, 98
        Oysters Rockefeller, 128
    redfish:
        Fish Tacos with Coastal Taco-lade Sauce, 36
        Pecan-Crusted Redfish, 115
        Redfish Sauce Piquante, 166
    shrimp:
        Basic Shrimp Stock, 108
        Crabmeat-Stuffed Shrimp, 92
        New Orleans Shrimp Étouffée, 78
        New Orleans-Style Barbecue Shrimp, 68
        Seafood Gumbo, 20
        Shrimp and Andouille Gumbo, 108
        Shrimp Creole, 65
        Shrimp Rémoulade, 66
        Stuffed Mirliton, 134
        Eggs Sardou, 70
    Trout Meunière, 117
Seafood Gumbo, 20
shallot:
    Creole Daube, 122
    Herbsaint Dressing, 130
    Larded Roast, 123

Trout Meunière, 117
sherry:
  Oyster and Artichoke Soup, 98
  Turtle Soup, 96
shrimp: see seafood
Shrimp and Andouille Gumbo, 108
Shrimp Creole, 65
Shrimp Rémoulade, 66
Slow Roasted Duck with Orange and Soy
  Sauce Gravy, 158
Smothered Creole Pork Roast, 165
Smothered Greens with Pecan-Smoked
  Bacon, 102
Soft Shell Crab Amandine, 90
soup:
  Oyster and Artichoke Soup, 98
  Turtle Soup, 96
Spaghetti Bordelaise, 125
Spareribs, Kevin's Dry and Wet Barbecue, 104
spinach:
  Creamed Spinach, 71
  Fried Oysters and Spinach Salad with
    Fresh Ponchatoula Strawberries, 130
  Oysters Rockefeller, 128
Steen's Pure Cane Syrup:
  Corn and Sweet Pepper Relish, 145
  Louisiana Pecan Pie, 137
  Nan's Saturday Buttermilk Pancakes
    with Praline Bacon Sprinkles, 48
  Sweet Potato Gnocchi with Sage and
    Feta, 150
  Traditional Creole Louisiana Pecan
    Praline, 80
Stock, Basic Shrimp, 108

Strawberries, Fried Oysters and Spinach
  Salad with Fresh Ponchatoula, 130
Stuffed Green Bell Peppers, 44
Stuffed Mirliton, 134
Sweet Potato Gnocchi with Sage and Feta, 150
Sweet Potato Pecan Casserole, 151
Sweet Potato Pie, 46

T

Tacos with Coastal Taco-lade Sauce, Fish, 36
Tartar Sauce, Creole, 119
Thin-Fried Beer-Battered Catfish, 118
Tiramisu Cupcakes, 86
tomato:
  Beef Rouladen, 59
  Chef Kevin's Jambalaya à la Big Easy, 32
  Chef Kevin's New Orleans-Glazed Ham
    Po'Boys, 50
  Creole Okra, 146
  Fried Green Tomatoes, 148
  Grillades and Grits, 26
  New Orleans Shrimp Étouffée, 78
  Red Gravy New Orleans Style, 83
  Redfish Sauce Piquante, 166
  Shrimp Creole, 65
  Stuffed Green Bell Peppers, 44
  Traditionally Classic Guacamole, 39
  Turtle Soup, 96
tomato sauce:
  Redfish Sauce Piquante, 166
  Stuffed Green Bell Peppers, 44
tortilla:
  Fish Tacos with Coastal Taco-lade
    Sauce, 36

Homemade Tortilla Crisps, 40
Traditional Creole Louisiana Pecan
  Praline, 80
Traditional New Orleans Calas, 31
Traditionally Classic Guacamole, 39
trinity, 16-17
Triple Threat Meatballs, 84
Trout Meunière, 117
turkey: see poultry
turnip, in Creole Daube, 122
Turtle Soup, 96

V

veal:
  Paneed Veal, 139
  Triple Threat Meatballs, 84

W

Whiskey Sauce, 143
White Rémoulade, 66
whole milk: see milk
wine:
  red wine:
    Beef Rouladen, 59
    Creole Cottage Pie, 160
    Creole Daube, 122
    Red Cabbage, 62
    Redfish Sauce Piquante, 166
  white wine:
    Basic Shrimp Stock, 108
    Brabant Potatoes, 155
    Chicken Clemenceau, 155
    Lorna's Oyster Patties, 127
    Spaghetti Bordelaise, 125
    Trout Meunière, 117

METRIC CONVERSION CHART

Volume Measurements		Weight Measurements		Temperature Conversion	
U.S.	**Metric**	**U.S.**	**Metric**	**Fahrenheit**	**Celsius**
1 teaspoon	5 ml	1/2 ounce	15 g	250	120
1 tablespoon	15 ml	1 ounce	30 g	300	150
1/4 cup	60 ml	3 ounces	90 g	325	160
1/3 cup	75 ml	4 ounces	115 g	350	180
1/2 cup	125 ml	8 ounces	225 g	375	190
2/3 cup	150 ml	12 ounces	350 g	400	200
3/4 cup	175 ml	1 pound	450 g	425	220
1 cup	250 ml	2 1/4 pounds	1 kg	450	230

KEVIN BELTON

Kevin Belton, a teacher of the fundamentals of Louisiana cooking for more than twenty years, is an instructor at The New Orleans School of Cooking, and has been recognized as one of the top thirty Louisiana chefs by the American Culinary Federation. Belton explores the distinctive Creole food of New Orleans in his PBS cooking series, *New Orleans Cooking with Kevin Belton*, which will begin airing in the spring of 2016. He also appeared in a series produced by the BBC called *Big Kevin, Little Kevin*. Kevin has been a guest on numerous food programs including *Emeril Live, Ready . . . Set . . . Cook!, Life, Love, and Lunch, Taste of America*, and *Food Fighters*. Belton's mission is to "get you to cook, and then to sit down with your family or invite a friend over and share that meal."

RHONDA K. FINDLEY

Rhonda K. Findley is the coauthor of several New Orleans-centric books including the best-selling *100 Greatest New Orleans Recipes of All Time* and *New Orleans Unleashed*. Her thirty-year culinary career includes professional restaurant management, radio broadcast, and freelance food writing. She also owns a historic coffee shop and operates her retail ventures, Funrock'n and Pop City, selling her original clothing and jewelry designs. She makes her home in the Bywater-Marigny neighborhood of New Orleans with her 9th Ward dogs, Presston, Reni, and Mr. Big Stuff.